JAPAN'S

JAPAN'S SEX TRADE

A Journey Through Japan's Erotic Subcultures

by Peter Constantine

Charles E. Tuttle Company
Tokyo, Japan

Cover collage by Kasei Inoue

Published by the Charles E. Tuttle Company, Inc.
of Tokyo, Japan
with editorial offices at
2-6 Suido 1-chome, Bunkyo-ku, Tokyo 112

©1993 by Charles E. Tuttle Publishing Co., Inc.

LCC Card No. 93-60946
ISBN 0-8048-1922-x

First edition, 1994

Printed in Japan

CONTENTS

ACKNOWLEDGMENTS

Many of the individuals who were most instrumental in making *Japan's Sex Trade* possible have wished to remain anonymous. I am very thankful to them for having allowed me to grill and re-grill them on sensitive and sometimes even embarrassing details of their current or former work. I could not have written this book without the mass of information that they agreed to share.

I am especially grateful to K. Inoue for his tireless help in digging out and analyzing mountains of material. His clear understanding of the ins and outs of the Japanese scene were of enormous help. I am also very grateful to W. Ishida, whose deep knowledge of Japan's culture, past and present, brought into perspective some of the more idiosyncratic twists of red-light life, and to Greg Allen for his social and linguistic acumen.

I would like to thank T. Yoshioka for all the information she helped me gather over the past four years, and to express my appreciation for her insight into the forbidden language of Japan's sex-trade, and also for keeping her sharp eye on the blue press in Tokyo, Osaka, and Yokohama.

I would also like to thank my editor Sally Schwager for undertaking so many fact-finding missions for me, and for intercepting and interviewing important

Tokyo figures; and also Dr. Lundquist, chief librarian of the Oriental Division of the New York Public Library, Ms. Kim, section head of the East Asian Division, and their staff, for suggesting books and articles that provided vital information, and for their constant scholarly assistance; and my agent Raphael Pallais for his enthusiastic support.

Finally, a very special thank you to Burton Pike who inspired me to write my first book, *Japanese Street Slang*, and whose constant advice and constant encouragement over the years have made this book possible.

INTRODUCTION

My ultimate mission in *Japan's Sex Trade* was to explore the fascinating but prohibited side of Japan which, like the taboo language it speaks, is out of bounds to foreigners. In the mid-eighties I set off on a five-year linguistic expedition to capture the fiercest and slangiest expressions the Japanese street scene had to offer. I had begun with sampling the scintillating and private amphetamine and opium jargons of drug cliques, and then plowed my way through the lingo of the Koganechō brothels of Yokohama and the flashy Korean creole of the gangs of Kawasaki. Words poured in: words for guns, words for organs, words for pocket-picking techniques, words describing brothels, bathhouses, massage parlors, and S&M clubs. By 1991 I had gathered stacks upon stacks of notes and squeezed them into *Japanese Street Slang*, which came out the following year.

Even though my slang project was over, I was still going on nocturnal language missions, my tape recorder ready for action. Among the many new slang sources I was meeting in New York that year was a group of captivating women who had worked in some of the most notorious pink salons in Tokyo.

"*Geso* really means tentacles," the conversation would go, "like the legs of a squid. But in sushi bar lingo *geso* also means shoes. So when you're in a brothel, *geso warui!*—the tentacles are bad!—means that the shoes outside the rooms, like the men inside, are in bad shape. Forget the tip, ha, ha! Oh, yes, and *tsuē, dē, ēe,* means 'one', 'two', 'three', in striptease. Like, *atashi tsuē* means 'I'm on first'."

"Tell him about vacuum fellatio!"

These women were a slang collector's dream. Cackling, they would chat about "washing hair," "fruit dates," "flower time," and "bowling." Prices were compared, working methods discussed, and women from other red-light branches were bad-mouthed. Before I knew it I had dropped my notebook and was cross-examining my new victims about club fees, S&M registration, and the interior decoration of pink salon sex-booths. Were banquettes covered with leather? Were there tables, and didn't they get in the way? If there was just linoleum on the floor, wasn't it too slippery for specials like "upside-down pot service?"

A strange new world was beginning to unfold. I realized that throughout my years of collecting slang I had been so focused on what people said that I never thought about asking what they did while they were saying it. "A language-hunter hunts language—leave the rest to sociology!" had been my initial motto. But as more and more information came pouring in, the urge to organize it into book form became irresistible. As a precautionary measure, I was going to add a lexical subtitle along the lines of "language from the floating world."

The initial idea had been to stun the Western reader with long alphabetical lists that were meant to unravel the darkest practices of contemporary Japanese parlors, from massage, "health," and S&M clubs to the hard-core soapland bathhouses and the hustler bars. But more anecdotes, more confessions, more reminiscences came flooding in. I was also beginning to search for historical and legal background information. When exactly was the Anti-Prostitution Law passed? Who did what to circumvent it? How can Suzuko get away with what she does in her sex-booth and not be arrested for prostitution? At the Public Library in New York I came across interesting books like *Gendai no Baishun to Jinken* (Modern Prostitution and Human Rights), *Sekkusu to Yu Oshigoto* (Sex as Work), and *Sei no Ōkoku* (The Kingdom of Sex), which confirmed among other things some of the more outlandish tales I had heard about the sex factories of the Ogoto region.

As *Japan's Sex Trade* was taking shape, it was becoming increasingly less of a language book. I had decided to keep a sampling of the parlor menus—the step-by-step chronicling of what is for sale—but I was now determined to present as clear a picture as I could of this strange and exotic aspect of Japan.

1992 was a particularly interesting year for Japan's red-light scene. The economy had taken an unexpected plunge, and establishments rich and poor were being rattled to their foundations. "The bubble has burst!" everyone gasped. 1992 was also the big year of *dyūda*—changing from one sex-trade branch to another. Bathhouse masseuses were becoming S&M dominatrixes, health girls were switching to pink salons and back, and pink salon women were turning to image clubs, where to titillate their clients they would disguise themselves as nurses, high school girls, and housewives with aprons and curlers.

Debts were on the rise. Hostesses working in

Tokyo's exclusive Ginza District, multi-millionaires in the eighties, could now no longer pay off their credit-card charges. Some turned to prostitution (*tengai-dēto*, "outside-the-store dates"), others fled to Korea. Even the popular magazine *Asahi Geinō* reported in a February 1993 article the scandalous sight of hordes of crème-de-la-crème women scrambling out of bars, running hysterically to Ginza Station to catch the last train because they could no longer afford a cab home.

The sudden recession was affecting everybody. College girls and young secretaries who in the late eighties and early nineties had indulged in fast cars, fancy restaurants, and expensive apartments, now had to face the music. Hardest hit were the *shindarera furaito gyaru* (Cinderella flight girls). Even when the recession hit they refused to face reality. Right into the autumn of 1992, come Friday afternoon these girls would swarm out of their offices and head for the airports, ready for exotic weekend trips to Guam, Hong Kong, and even Hawaii. The *shirōto būmu* (amateur-boom) hit the parlors.

It was fascinating to witness the major day-to-day changes in the sex-trade arena as I was writing, interviewing, and probing throughout 1992 and 1993. AIDS consciousness was setting in; an impish bathhouse regular was making a name for himself on the Tokyo scene by confessing, as he left each establishment, that he had AIDS, and that even though you couldn't see it he was close to death. The women flipped out, and small but unmistakable changes appeared on parlor and brothel menus. Uncondomed services were rising in price, and most institutions now tested their women for HIV twice a month, plastering the walls with prominent health certificates. The Utagawa bath-house in Tokyo went even further. Customers who were paying $400 and $500 a session often flatly refused to wear condoms, but, given the go-ahead, became squeamish: "If you let everyone do it without, how do I know you don't have AIDS?" The director, Mr. Fukui Tatsuya, steered the establishment out of these dangerous waters by requiring his soap ladies to wear their blood test results pinned to their robes.

Another phenomenon of the early nineties was the frantic nationwide interest in sadomasochism. Practically every parlor joined in. Some went all the way and specialized in the newest and trendiest forms of bondage; others just quickly dressed a masseuse or two in leather and dispensed whips. But either way, *esu-emu* (S&M) successfully penetrated the fashion world, soap operas, and TV talk shows, clinching its popularity with the arrival of the Japanese version of Madonna's book *SEX* in December of 1992. S&M even invaded the temperate realms of Tokyo executive circles: "For the hottest date, get a 3-O girl! (*san-o-gyaru*)." Her first "O" stands for "office lady" (secretary), her second for *ojōsama* (princess, or in this case dominatrix), and her third and final "O" indicates that she has an *otaku* (a home, i.e. one does not have to take her to an expensive hotel to get whipped).

The biggest change on Japan's sex-trade scene was the withdrawal of the Yakuza, the Japanese mob. For years they had openly ruled every aspect of the red-light trade, from delivering napkins, towels, and tooth-picks to massage parlors, to deciding which women worked in what brothels and on what days. The Yakuza had imported the *Jappayuki* (Japan-bound) prostitutes from the Philippines, and later brought in batches of fresher women from Thailand. They had set up and conducted the multi-billion dollar sex-tour business in Bangkok, and then, with the AIDS scare, shifted their trade to the more innocent territories of Vietnam. But sharp new anti-mob laws loosened the Yakuza's grip on Japan's modern pleasure quarters, and the tough men with their full-body tattoos have, for the time being, disappeared from the street corners, the slummy dark entrances of the sex-parlors, the salons, and the clubs.

As my writing continued I decided to add color to the different segments of the sex-trade world by introducing, as a backdrop, Japan's peculiar pornographic scene. In a country where an acrobatic soap lady might service naked clients while swinging from the ceiling, and where agencies like Shibuya Dicks and Come Boy guarantee delivery of a male hustler in 20 minutes, too much pubic hair shown in a magazine can still unleash a scandalized police raid. Video directors like Muranishi Tōru and Haga Eitarō fought hard to show as much action as possible through the obfuscating *mozaiku* (mosaic) which by law had to completely blot out offending organs. As a conciliatory gesture, the authorities would look the other way whenever the mosaic was turned on one or two seconds too late, giving viewers the chance to quickly freeze the scene by pressing the still-button on their remote controls. Companies like KK Club and Best Selection began to distribute complex anti-censorship machines to outwit the mosaic. One of the cheaper $100 contraptions, *mosaic non*, comes in a square box. Its drawback is that it must be held, like binoculars, to the viewer's eyes. Many customers complain that what with the remote in one hand and the *mosaic non* in the other, relaxing with a video is becoming quite a cumbersome task. Other more expensive models, like the $350 Super Killer-VC88 and the $650 Super Eight Special, afforded more freedom, as they can be plugged directly into the television system.

In *Japanese Street Slang* I had tried to display the beautiful and rich street languages of the slums of Tokyo, Osaka, Kawasaki, and Utsunomiya, along with secret word histories and elusive etymologies. In *Japan's Sex Trade* my basic goal has been simpler. I wanted to guide the reader past the prominent No Foreigners! signs on the entrance of S&M clubs, gay bars, soaplands and anal-massage parlors, second-hand-panty boutiques, and sex shops, and to unveil a very human, but very different Japan.

1 • WOMEN WITH RED LAMPS

When the Anti-Prostitution Law descended on Japan in 1957, some of the lower red-light echelons with firm roots in the slums and shanty towns of large cities refused to budge. At first, mass hysteria broke out as retired prostitutes, pimps, and small-time mobsters realized that the government meant business about closing down their mini-brothels and the red-light bars into which they had sunk their life's savings. They protested, picketed, and committed little acts of terrorism, but when it became clear that the Draconian law was here to stay, they put their heads together and decided that they would close down their houses of ill repute and immediately re-open them as something else. The brothel owners rushed down to their local police stations, and as their houses were struck off the register one by one, "restaurants" sprang up in their stead. Food, however, was remarkably absent from their menus.

There is an area of Yokohama, in one of the rougher neighborhoods near the port, that has remained to this day among Japan's most blatant brothel quarters. As one walks from the Isezaki District up towards the railroad tracks beyond the Ōka River that runs down into the harbor, bright posters set up by the local police warn "Beware of AIDS!" and "Beware of Violent Criminals!" and, in what looks like a desperate appeal to the neighborhood, "Stop Foreign Prostitutes!" In the dead of night soft Philippine and Thai voices call out from dim street corners, "Choi no ma?" (Wanna quickie?) as dump trucks and tired cabs cruise slowly past. Just across the river in Koganechō, a two-block mini-district that stretches under the elevated railroad tracks, 180 small brothels that defied the law back in 1956 have remained open. The dilapidated two-floor shanties of wood and corrugated iron, made to measure under the tracks along the 500-odd yards of Koganechō, rattle when the train passes overhead. The girls stand waiting in the doorways. A 15-minute session costs between $90 and $100.

In the early fifties, Koganechō and the two blocks of neighboring Shiroganechō were one of the newer unlicensed prostitution areas that had sprung up in the desperate years after World War II. The elevated tracks had been built in 1931 for the Shonan Electric Railroad, and by the following year 990 people were living under them. During the allied bombing raids in 1945, Koganechō's railroad bridge became a death-trap for thousands when everything under and around it went up in flames. In the next few years dumpy bars and grungy noodle shops appeared, and along with them the ¥200 prostitutes.

The early Koganechō brothels had a set layout. A seedy bar on the street side with the owner and his family living in the back room, and on the second floor, right under the tracks, the two or three small rooms in which the prostitutes worked. The owners did well for themselves, especially after the Anti-Prostitution Law was passed, and soon the bars and noodle shops were being shut down to make more rooms that could be rented at a boisterous profit to new prostitutes. But even more rental rooms were needed, and by the late sixties and throughout the seventies the owners and their families started moving to better neighborhoods so they could subdivide whole ground floor areas into small and expensive cubicles. By 1980, the official resident count of Koganechō had dropped to 95 people.

By the late eighties, Taiwanese and Philippine prostitutes started appearing in the brothels and on the street corners, followed in the early nineties by a wave of Thai girls. With them came a new pimping-husband phenomenon, in which the prostitute would marry—paying her husband an average of $500 a month—so that she could legally remain in Japan. The girls soon realized that being a foreigner in Koganechō was expensive; by 1993, the room rates had rocketed to as much as $1,000 a month. The landlords, however, possibly in compliance with the police posters, rented out the rooms exclusively to bona fide Japanese girls or to pimp-brokers who charged the foreign girls anywhere from $4,000 to $6,000 a month.

In a December, 1992 interview with *Marco Polo* magazine Mr. Hattori, head of the Koganechō Restaurant and Bar Association, commented on how the foreign girls had boosted the Koganechō economy by working for the brothels at a fraction of what Japanese prostitutes would work for. The Taiwanese girls who had come in a wave in the mid-eighties, he continued, were now all in their early thirties and somewhat "past it," and it was the rush of teenage Thai prostitutes in the 1990s that whipped new life into the streets.

The police have recently gone beyond their poster-pasting campaign, and have begun storming the brothels. In a 1991 onslaught, 156 prostitutes were dragged to the precinct, 118 of them Thai. In a January, 1992 raid, 80 more were arrested. Then a Thai girl got AIDS and was sent back to Thailand in disgrace, and new posters were put up throughout the area.

Another infamous area where brothels were quickly turned into restaurants on the eve of the Anti-Prostitution Law was Tobita in Osaka's Nishinari District. Tobita has more of a sensational past than its sister district in Yokohama. It had started off in the early 1600s as one of Osaka's seven cemeteries, and became notorious by doubling as a feared center to which Osaka criminals were dragged for execution. In the 1860s the cemetery moved east to the Abeno District, the execution center was closed down, and Tobita turned into a bustling slum.

Its career as a red-light district started in 1914 when a flash fire totally wrecked Minami, the most prominent red-light district in *fin-de-siècle* Osaka, just a mile north of Tobita. The rich but now destitute brothel owners were frantically scouting for prime brothel real estate. The consensus was that the new turf would have be close enough to Minami to keep old clients coming, but far enough from the charred ruins and the devastated roads and bridges to be easily accessible. The new territory, everyone agreed, had to be cheap. Tobita was the obvious choice, and in 1919 the first brothel opened, after much exorcism, pomp, and ceremony, on the grounds of the former cemetery. The neighborhood was scandalized and took to the streets in protest, but the Minami brothel owners had quickly formed the Hannan Real Estate

Company and had systematically bought up the whole area.

Rows of brothels opened, and the Tobita red-light district stretched from Sanno and Tengachaya into the neighboring Tennoji District. Business was so good that desperate brothel owners even snatched up the northeastern corner of the Abeno Cemetery.

In 1928, the arrival of the Nankai Hirano Railroad clinched Tobita's red-light supremacy. The tracks were only five miles long and ran from Imaike, just outside Tobita, to the old Nankai Hirano Station. But now Tobita was accessible from all directions, and eager men cascaded in from surrounding districts. Two years later, by 1930, the brothel count was up to 220, with the prostitute count at a dizzying 2,700.

As the Anti-Prostitution Law went into effect on April Fools' Day in 1957, Tobita's rows of brothels, like those in Yokohama, hastily transformed themselves into *ryōtei* (restaurants), with the prostitutes changing into *arubaito no jokyu* (part-time waitresses). That same year, the government set up its first prostitute rehabilitation center in Tennoji, and although the prostitutes were slow in flocking in, a second center was set up the following year in nearby Nishinari. The brothels, aware of the delicacy of the situation, immediately protected themselves by forming a powerful "restaurant" association, which started working closely with the local mob and the police. The solidarity among the Tobita owners became so strong that all the brothel prices, services, and even the decor were standardized.

While the Yokohama brothels are a blend of concrete, corrugated iron, and wood, Tobita prides itself on sustaining the pre-war wooden *yūkaku* (brothel)

look. The association put much effort into steering clear from Tobita's dangerous former image of being among Osaka's largest red-light centers, and worked on publicly redefining itself as a *shoten-gai* (shopping center). It was common knowledge, however, that nothing had changed, and in 1960 the then young tabloid, *Shūkan Taishū*, proclaimed to the world that a beer, a snack, and a 40-minute session was available at any of the old Tobita haunts for ¥700. By the end of that year 3,164 Osaka prostitutes and pimps were dragged down to the precinct.

These days most of the action takes place after midnight. Walking around the blocks with their 150 brothels, the unsuspecting pedestrian might think he is in a quaint late-night noodle shop district, with row upon row of tiny weatherworn restaurants conveniently huddled one next to the other. As he looks in, past the colorful and short *noren* curtains hanging over the top half of the door, he will see an elderly lady in a kimono kneeling silently on a cushion next to a girl he might mistake for her fashion-conscious granddaughter. The pedestrian's suspicions, however, might be aroused as he peeks into the next store and sees yet another traditional matriarch with another young companion, and then further down another and another. As he walks back up the block in confusion, he notices that men are disappearing off the street to be led up staircases by the old women.

Each house has three or four girls who are organized into strict shifts by the elderly woman downstairs. The girls come down from their rooms to sit beside her one at a time, in five-minute shifts, so that passersby, wandering up and down the block, can see who is available. When a client enters the brothel the old lady jumps into action. She bustles about, bowing and uttering pleasantries, asking the client to follow her upstairs so she can "serve him a drink." The silent rule among Tobita madames is never to mention prices or sex before they have dragged the customer to the safety of the second floor. Once upstairs the charade is over, and the old lady rattles down the price list: a 20-minute quickie, $100; half an hour, $200; 40 minutes $250. "All our girls are healthy— here are the weekly blood-test results."

WATAKANO ISLAND

Japan's most brazen center of prostitution lies hidden in a distant corner of the Ise-shima National Park on Watakano, a tranquil and beautiful little island just off the Pacific coast. Watakano has remained the best-kept Japanese sex-trade secret, jealously nurtured by the Yakuza mob, which, since the Anti-Prostitution Law of 1957, has strictly guarded the Matoya Bay area in which the island lies. Men who travel to the national park for a two-day stay at the island's brothels arrive in groups at Anakawa Station on the Kintetsu-shima line. They have all made reservations in advance, and must state their name and city of origin before they can climb into the Yakuza-monitored vessel which will ferry them half a mile across the bay to the island. As they board, a guard with a cellular phone calls the brothels to confirm the guest list, and bogus customers, reporters, and policemen are dragged off the boat.

The island is flat and green, triangular in shape. It has 14 hotels, 23 red-light bars, and 200 prostitutes. The origin of the name of Watakano is a matter of heated dispute. Some of the prostitutes maintain that *wata-ka-no* should be written with the characters for "swimming over to set fire to the fields," while others contest this and use the more romantic characters "deer swim over to the fields."

As the boat docks at the concrete pier small parties of women wave energetically to welcome the clients.

WATAKANO—THE EARLY YEARS

Watakano Island has been a distinguished center of prostitution since the early seventeenth century. Legend has it that an impoverished faith-healer saved the dying daughter of Iemitsu, the third Shogun of Edo, shortly after he had come to power in 1623.

"Ask anything of me and it shall be granted!" the islanders report the grateful Shogun to have declared. So the faith-healer, kneeling before the ruler on an exquisite mat, requested 2,000 prostitutes and a license to set up brothels in the bays around Watakano, which lay strategically on the sea route halfway between Japan's largest medieval trading centers, Osaka and Edo (today's Tokyo). In those days, lines of fragile sailing vessels traveled cautiously from inlet to inlet, putting in at the slightest sign of a storm, and the bored sailors would sit on beaches in somber groups, their pockets full of freshly earned coins. The faith-healer changed all that. According to the islanders, the Shogun bought up the daughters and young wives of impoverished local families, and set up a splendid string of sea-view brothels all the way from Toba to Matoya.

These women became the first *funajorō* (ship whores) of the area. In the early days they were known as the *sentakunin* (washer-women). Housewives in need of extra cash would carefully fold all their finery into a bundle and, leaving for Matoya Bay, would explain to the neighbors that they were going down to the sea to do their washing. The direct forerunners of today's island prostitutes were mysteriously known as *hashirigane*, the etymology of which, after more than three centuries, is still unresolved on Watakano Island. Some of the women believe that whenever their predecessors saw a large ship they would *hashiri* (run) down to the beach, hastily throwing on their *gane* (the "metal" or jewelry they wore to work). Other women interpret *hashirigane* to mean "running crab": the prostitutes ran out onto the beach, shuffling like crabs in their tight kimonos and their clattering wooden *geta* sandals. Still others argue that their predecessors' name meant "fresh money"—they would snatch up a sailor's cash before he could spend it elsewhere—while a more conservative group maintains that *hashirigane* means "running needles." In the old days the prostitutes were very domestic, and would patch up their customer's clothes by running needles through them.

Today's women stay on the island, walking between the snackbars where they meet the clients and the hotels where they entertain them. The *hashirigane* of yesteryear were much more enterprising. Before the sailors had a chance to disembark, women would climb into a *choro*, a small wooden rowboat, and a villager known as a *kogoshi*, basically a pimp, would row from ship to ship as the men whistled and howled. The *hashirigane* separated themselves into three categories: *anejorō*, the senior women, more elegant, beautiful, and accomplished; the younger *wakajorō;* and the novices, the *pinkoro*. They scrambled onto the ships according to their rank and took position, the *anejorō* in the center where they could be admired from all angles, the younger *wakajorō* at the sides, and the youngest well out of the way by the ship's bow. When everyone was safely on board the women loosened their *obi* (sashes), stepped out of their kimonos, and struck elegant poses.

The *hashirigane* prospered for three centuries. Watakano islanders remember with nostalgia romantic tales of prostitutes of the most squalid backgrounds who married rich captains and moved to the capital to become respected matrons. At the height of the trade boom of the late nineteenth century rows of ships were docked next to each other, so that an enterprising *hashirigane* could hoist herself from deck to deck working her way from Watakano across the bays to Anori.

Prostitutes split up into factions to deal with the mounting workload. Super-elite women remained in their exclusive boudoirs on the island and took calls from captains and wealthy merchants. The less powerful *hashirigane* who still had to ride out to the boats came to be known as *noriko* (riding girls). Astute businesswomen, they carefully selected the boats they would target; with the unfortunate boom in the dung-trade between Edo and Osaka, they steered clear of the clumps of grungier vessels. The dung-merchants were serviced by desperate prostitutes who were referred to by their more successful colleagues as *guso* (shits).

THE LAST OF THE HASHIRIGANE

At the beginning of the twentieth century the era of the sailing vessel came to an end. Large and powerful ships set their sights on international ports, and horrified prostitutes saw all their old customers steam right past the bays. The panicking women were saved by the Suzuki Corporation in Kobe City, which built a gigantic shipyard in the area, bringing in thousands upon thousands of workers. The *hashirigane* left the beaches and settled inland.

On Watakano Island brothels such as Yokarō, Kinseirō, and Tomoerō soon came into their own, and nightly parties were arranged in the dining rooms of Osakaya and Takashimaya, the island's main hotels.

Even respectable local women energetically chipped in to work as hostesses, pouring drinks and fluttering around the hard-working shipbuilders. In 1927, however, disaster struck. The shipyard was abruptly dismantled, its more than 10,000 shocked workers sent home and, for the first time in more than three centuries, the whole area tumbled into severe economic depression.

The Anori Village, a few miles north of Watakano Island, reverted to fishing and dedicated itself to developing the Anori Bunraku puppet theater, which was to become famous throughout Japan. The Matoya Village, on the mainland near Watakano, devoted itself to oyster fishing, turning its special breed of *matoya-kaki* (matoya-oyster) into a national delicacy. By 1932 there was only one brothel left, with five weary *hashirigane*. Toba Bay, a few miles north, still had five brothels and 40 prostitutes; there the railroad had already arrived, bringing with it the first tourists who were quickly followed by pearl merchants responsible for helping the villagers set up the famous Toba pearl farms.

The prostitutes on Watakano Island were virtually the only ones to survive unscathed. In a 1932 essay, writer and social historian Iwata Junichi comments on the beauty of the island, a place "where it is eternal spring." He writes of the boat trip from Anakawa Station, which in those days took 45 minutes, and bemoans the end of an era. In particular Iwata Junichi describes his emotion at the historically significant sight of the 1930s *hashirigane* flocking, as their mothers and grandmothers had done long before them, down to the wooden pier to greet the men on the arriving ferry.

WATAKANO ISLAND—THE 1990s

The men start arriving on the island in the afternoon and are helped off the boat by the women waiting on the pier in their fashionable and expensive outfits. The island is very small; its coastline is only five miles around, so the men split into groups and hastily walk to their hotels to prepare themselves for the big *enkai* (meeting-party). Those who do look around are struck by the beauty and tranquility of the natural setting. The men check into the hotels, and the staff closely examines their papers. The uninitiated client is surprised at the absence of a bed in his room. Puzzled, he might ask the maid, who explains *sotto voce* that protocol on the island dictates that any young lady or ladies he meets will take him to a *bijinesu hoteru* (business hotel). This way everything stays nice and proper, especially if during the night the police de-

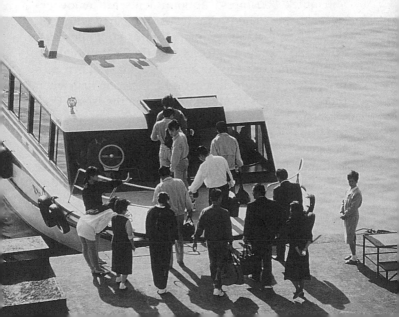

cide to launch an aquatic offensive from Matoya or Sangasho.

The men spend the afternoon relaxing and strolling about comfortably in their casual *yukata* robes and their wooden clogs—the big meeting-party is scheduled from six to eight in the evening. Those impatient to meet women immediately go to a "snack," a red-light bar. To the untrained eye the bar-counter just happens to be filled with happy young women, many of them from the Philippines and Thailand, all eager to meet men. Clients point, the women take an immediate liking to them, and they leave arm in arm for a "business" hotel. The smooth tryst costs the customer $100 for 20 minutes, a percentage of which the prostitute pays back to the "snack" that secretly employs her.

The real action on Watakano Island takes place at the meeting-parties. For a $100 *anshin ryō* (relief fee), hordes of men get to mingle with hordes of women, and quick "business" appointments are made between drinks. The prostitutes at the party will book themselves for a series of half-hour stints between 8p.m. and 11p.m., and then go for the $350 all-nighter, lasting from 11p.m. to the morning. This system comes in handy, especially during the high-season rush when there are always many more men on the island than women.

Since the early fifties, the Watakano enterprise has been very nervous about the possibility of being infiltrated and uncovered by the press. In December of 1992, the young Tokyo journalist Mihiro Kuruto, along with photographer Miyajima Shigeki, finally broke through the anti-press barriers and exposed the island in a *Marco Polo* magazine special. Mihiro Kuruto writes candidly of following a "snack" woman to her "business" hotel where she checks his papers (to make sure he is not a policeman or, worse, a member of the press). He reports his surprise at finding that all room doors are wide open, regardless of whether customers are in session or not, and that as an extra safety measure, an elderly woman shamelessly darts in and out of the rooms.

The weekend following the article's publication, lines of cars converged on the province of Mie. The furious local Yakuza mob tightened its security net around Watakano, thanking providence that the annoying article had been vague about the exact whereabouts of the tiny island. Fortunately the dangerous exposé had appeared during the deepest winter months, when snow, rain, and long office hours kept even the keenest city-dwellers at bay. Only the hardiest of tourists found their way to Matoya, and they were brushed off at the pier with a "Go away, we're booked!"

Back in Tokyo, Mihiro Kuruto was snubbed and attacked by fellow journalists and panicky patrons of Watakano. Writer and cartoonist Nemoto even attacked *Marco Polo* magazine and Kuruto in a furious article in *SPA* magazine within days of the exposé. Why did they have to use the island's real name? Three hundred years of hallowed tradition blown away!

2 • SOAPLANDS

If a man wishes his body to be professionally washed, steamed, licked, and manipulated to orgasm, and is prepared to pay between $100 and $850, he might turn to a soap lady working in one of Japan's many notorious soaplands. Of all the sex-trade establishments, the soaplands offer the most ingenious and far-reaching array of sexual services for sale in Japan today. They skillfully dodge the Anti-Prostitution Law by operating under the camouflage of body-washing and massaging.

The soapland "menu" has been a favorite in Japan since the early Kamakura Period, when bathhouses of ill repute offered masseuses in the two categories of *oyuna* (big hot-water-females) for the senior specialists, and their novices, usually 12- to 15-years-old, known as *koyuna* (small hot-water-females). In the decade after World War II this type of bathhouse adopted the more fashionable name *Toruko-buro* (Turkish bath), offering the man in the street a cheaper, quicker, and often more relaxing alternative to an all-out bordello. The big and small hot-water-females were renamed *Toruko-jo* (Turkish girls).

In those days poverty was rampant. Times were so rough that even respectable housewives took to the streets as *matchi uri no shojo* (match-selling girls). For a yen they would strike a match, lift up their skirts, and

33

yank down their bloomers. When the match went out, the peeking time was over and bloomers were hoisted. Times being what they were, bathhouses of every persuasion were flooded by waves of destitute women who hoped to end up as masseuses rather than selling matches or working in brothels. In the brothels as *baishunfu* ("spring-selling girls" or prostitutes), they would be expected to sell "spring" to a minimum of 12 men per shift, and up to a staggering maximum of 60. So many eager masseuses were available that even the reputable Tokyo Onsen (Tokyo Hot Spring) opened up a whole floor of private massage rooms. As the red-light world in those post-war days was filled with desperate amateurs, the services were scanty compared with the ingenious and devious offerings available today.

Paradoxically, it took a major catastrophe, the Anti-Prostitution Law of 1957, to transform the bathhouse industry of yesteryear into the sophisticated institution it is now. This law shook the red-light districts all over the country to their foundations. Outraged prostitutes and their pimps protested loudly, sent petitions to the government, and even marched through the streets of Tokyo chanting "Auld Lang Syne," but to no avail. The law passed, and some half-million prostitutes ended up on the street. But not for long. Ever adaptable and courageous in the face of disaster, the sex houses reopened, not as brothels but as bona fide massage parlors and Turkish baths.

Back in 1951 Tokyo Hot Spring had introduced the first Miss *Toruko* (Miss Turkish), who coyly kneaded away in good clean fun, clicking her tongue and wagging her finger if her victims became too responsive. Miss *Toruko* was so wildly successful that by the mid-fifties, red-light magnates fleeing the Anti-Prostitution Law opened the first *Toruko* baths in Tokyo's Asakusa and Shinjuku Districts.

For the next 30 years the Turkish bath industry flourished throughout the country, changing the appearance of former red-light districts with its lurid, imaginative architecture. By 1963, 390 *Toruko* had sprouted up, and by 1966 the number had surged to 675, with 973 Miss *Toruko*. To keep customers interested, the bathhouses became bigger and better. Architects modeled the facades after Shogun fortresses, the Tower of London, Las Vegas casinos, and even gothic castles—sometimes bulldozing many styles into one. To ward off competition from other red-light enterprises, the Turkish girls were encouraged to expand their repertory by inventing ever more titillating "washes." By the mid-sixties, "hard service" had become the norm. First came *daburu purē* (double play), fellatio with optional cunnilingus, and by 1970 all Turkish establishments had graduated to *homban* (performance), the professional euphemism for straight-out sex.

The seventies proved to be the decade of daring inventions. The newer Turkish baths of Kawasaki City and Horinouchi introduced the rectangular inflatable airmat, on which the customers could lie while the Turkish girls swashed about with bubbles, soaps, and suds. *Matto sābisu* (mat service) revolutionized the scope of the *Toruko*; since the women were no longer constrained by the dangerously slippery tubs, a mountain of new washes became available. Square mats became the rage, then triangular mats, the newest invention being the *enkei matto*, a special "circle" mat that originated in a Gifu City bath called Kiyōshi (Prince). Another major invention that began in the baths in Horinouchi in the seventies and has remained an important part of today's nation-wide soapland service was the *senbōkyō* (periscope). After the initial rub-down and wash, the woman springs into the tub with the customer, wedges her arms under his thighs, and lifting him a few inches so that his organ "periscopes" out of the water, bends forward to reach it with her lips. In later variations, the woman remains outside the tub and services her customer by taking deep breaths and plunging her head into the sudsy bath water. Some *Toruko* developed the periscope theme even further offering *sakasa senbōkyō* (upside-down periscope) and *gyaku senbōkyō* (reverse periscope). The woman takes off her panties and climbs into a precarious upside-down position on the tub with her feet securely wedged on its plastic-lamé rim. Balancing herself by pressing her buttocks and thighs over the customer's head, she leans forward and performs the periscope special.

Another hit that began in Kawasaki City was the *sukebe isu* (pervert chair), followed by the pink chair, the dream chair, and the miracle chair. These chairs were made of plastic and were usually covered with intricate gold-lamé patterns. They had two adjacent seats with holes in the front and in the bottom so that the Turkish girl could sit comfortably in front of her customer, with easy access to his genitals and anus from various angles. These chairs were wildly popular and brought about a nationwide explosion of "pervert" specials, "pink" washes, "dream" services, and "miracle" games. Every Turkish bath equipped itself with the wonder chairs, and women were encouraged to be as acrobatic and as innovative as possible on them. But the customers wanted more, and the next sensation on the bath scene was the *mokuba* (wooden horse), which allowed the women even more flexibility, as they could now offer a jolty, see-saw type wash. The clients came in droves.

Times for the bath industry, however, were not always easy. Angry housewives picketed, and the government passed a law in 1964 that targeted both "locked-door massage" and nude Turkish girls. The Japan Bath Association panicked, but ever ready to adapt, its members unanimously decided that henceforth massage-doors would remain unlocked but firmly closed, and that all Turkish girls should be urged to keep on at least their waterproof massage-aprons—that is, if the customer did not mind too much. Then, in 1971, the Bath Association had an even closer shave. Eleven militant women members of Japan's House of Councilors submitted, entirely without warning, a proposal to illegalize private-room massage in all bathhouses. Before the *Toruko* magnates could retaliate, the powerful Nihon Bengoshi Rengōkai (Japan Lawyer Association) joined in, and officially pronounced Turkish massage to be blatant prostitution, and thus technically illegal. *Josei no sābisu* (women's service), they argued, had to be banned. The magnates frantically pulled strings in high places, and a major red-light crisis was averted in the nick of time. Professional sex-massage flourished, and by 1984 Japan could boast 3,094 Turkish baths and related massage parlors.

The soaplands we know today burst onto the scene in 1985, under the most bizarre circumstances. The Japan Bath Association was preparing to celebrate its thirtieth prosperous year of unimpeded body-washing, when fate struck an underhanded blow. Japan and Turkey had decided to embrace each other in friendship, and things Turkish suddenly became fashionable. Japan initiated major investments in Turkey, while cultural and industrial exchanges took place between the two nations. Things were going splendidly until a Turkish scholar, Nusert Sanjakli, set off on a newspaper campaign to denounce Japan's Turkish girls and the so-called Turkish baths they worked in. *Toruko* (Turkey), he vehemently complained, had become the Japanese word for "brothel," and *Toruko-jo* (Turkish girl) an outrageous and unacceptable synonym for "whore." This was a direct insult to Turkey and Turkey's maidens.

The Japanese government was most embarrassed. To avert a possible chill between the two nations, Japan immediately outlawed the Turkish baths and their girls. The stunned Japan Bath Association was faced with the choice of closing down or doing what it had done back in 1956—renaming itself. Its survival instincts intact, it launched a national "Find a New Name" contest. The winner, unanimously chosen from among 2,200 finalists, was the crisp, clean, wholesome-but-gamy "soapland." The banned Turkish girls were immediately reintroduced as *sōpu-jo* (soap girls), or more fashionably *sōpu-rēdi* (soap ladies). Within days, the irate Turkish bath owners had changed their neon signs, their advertising, and their calling cards, complaining loudly into the ubiquitous television cameras about the government, the price of neon, and impending doom.

But worse was yet to come. The sharp blow that Turkey had dealt the Japanese bathhouse industry was accompanied by an unexpected local attack: the revision of the Law on Businesses Affecting Public Morals, which took effect in February 1985, on Valentine's Day, no less. The new, freshly decorated soaplands now had to register with the Public Safety Commission, exposing themselves to possible police measures. To the Japan Bath Association's horror, the new law also disallowed the hiring of minors, which made a major dent in the service menus of soaplands that specialized in *rorikon sābisu* (Lolita-complex service). Under the new law, anyone caught hiring an adolescent girl or providing sex-massage to an adolescent boy ran the risk of being closed down for eight months. The doormen were also dealt with harshly. Even on the slowest days, a desperate doorman relying on a per head commission for his livelihood could not resort to dragging clients onto the premises against their will. The harshest blow, however, was the curtailing of all-night partying. Soaplands would now have to be locked up by midnight.

The Japanese police meant business. That same year, more than 6,500 people (6,575, to be exact) were arrested for trying to break this law, and many of the most seasoned soapland and massage parlor owners broke down under the strain and closed up shop. In Tokyo alone, by Valentine's Day, 1986—exactly one year after the law took effect—38 of 281 massage parlors had gone out of business.

The result of the turbulent eighties was to make the soapland world of the nineties tougher, more flexible, and better equipped to fight for its clientele with competing sex-bars, -clubs, and -cabarets. Many soaplands have placed greater emphasis on catchy theme decor. Tokyo's Ichiriki Chaya (Topnotch Tea House), for instance, specializes in medieval Japan.

The soap ladies wear formal kimonos, are well drilled in the complexities of tea ceremony, and perform their washes to the elegant sounds of the koto. Another Tokyo soapland, Yangu Redii (Young Lady), is known for its wild *kanja purē* (patient play) with nurses in starched uniforms. On New Year's Day the Yangu Redii customer receives a pretty embroidered pouch with a single pubic hair from his favorite nurse in it. Other places offer soap ladies disguised as airline hostesses, executive secretaries, and elementary or high school girls (who are actually safely in their twenties). Some soaplands take "themes" even further, punishing naughty customers with enemas, or changing the more eccentric client's diapers.

The nineties have also brought with them a flourish of larger and kinkier soaplands in the provinces. These sprang up after the harsh St. Valentine laws of 1985, which included a very strict zoning clause. New bathhouses, it stated, would not be permitted within 100 yards of schools, sports facilities, libraries, or child-welfare establishments. Some Japanese cities, in deference to the sick, even went so far as to add hospitals to the list. Soapland speculation ground to a halt. As a gesture of open-mindedness, however, the government allowed the opening of new establishments in the nation's old red-light areas, such as Tokyo's Yoshiwara, Kyoto's Gion, Osaka's Shinmachi, and Hakata's Nakasu. But the Japan Bath Association was not mollified. They complained that downtown real estate had so rocketed in price that no one could afford the space a respectable soapland would require. Furthermore, they would be beset by bars, clubs, and parlors of every denomination, and would have to fight for their lives. But the government refused to budge. As a result, soapland entrepreneurs left town and built newer, bigger, and brighter establishments on inter-city highways and in unfashionable industrial suburbs.

In the early nineties a surprise recession hit Japan and many middle-priced soaplands hit the skids and had to offer bargain washes and become what is known today as a *kakuyasu sōpu* (bargain soap). The prices of the most successful and exclusive of Tokyo's 257 soaplands, however, have not been affected by the recession and have continued to rise unhampered. In Yoshiwara, Tokyo's ancient red-light district, there are no fewer than 80 luxury soaplands that do not wash their clients for less than $450. The soap ladies there are models between jobs and triple-X video stars, and the bath areas in which they wash their customers have extra bedrooms, living rooms, and private bar facilities in which regulars can keep their own whiskey bottles. Clients can arrive and leave in a chauffeur-driven Mercedes, unless they

specifically request something more discreet like a Toyota. While the cheap soapland hands out loud business cards, often pink in color with beckoning naked women, a classy establishment will sport the logo of a reputable bank, with the woman's name subtitled with "Section Chief" or "International Representative."

Tokyo's most expensive soapland is Shangrila, where the two-hour specials start at $750. A few streets down Saten Dōru (Satin Doll), Kurabu Enjoi (Club Enjoy), and Mink start at $700, while Gurando Kanyon (Grand Canyon) and Ginbasha (Silver Carriage) are a close third at $650. Business has been so steady at these cream-of-the-crop establishments that a new super-chic soapland, Maharaja Tokyo, opened with a flourish in Tokyo's Yoshiwara on New Year's Day 1993, offering a special two-hour wash for $550. The red-light crowd was stunned that a place of such grand proportions would dare to set up shop right in the middle of Japan's darkest recession in years—and that within walking distance of Yoshiwara's other 160 soaplands.

All soaplands, rich and poor, have had to extend their service menus. There is no limit to the extremes a modern hard-line soap lady will go to titillate her client—the more imaginative and delicate her touch, the more money she can extract from her client. From northern Hokkaido to southern Okinawa, soap ladies are encouraged to come up with new specialties, using tongues, breasts, knees, and toes in ever more creative ways. Like any other Japanese employer, the soapland is quick to spot good workers who throw themselves into their jobs, and dexterous women are given quick promotions and incentives like better "private rooms" and the highly fought-over titles of "Senior Soap Lady" and "Number One Body-Washer."

Soaplands increasingly present their massage-and-wash extravaganzas with the fanfare of an elite restaurant displaying its prized dishes. There is a growing trend to equate a delicate palate with delicate physical sensations. Sex-massages and body-washes appear under titles like *furu kōsu* (full course) or *osupe* (special, as in "special of the day"), sometimes coming out even more mysteriously as *sanshoku sushi* (triple-combo sushi) or *osashimi moriawase* (sashimi deluxe). Massage menus offer the customer the choice of a range of services that become progressively more expensive the more outlandish they are. The basic prix fixe bath fee averages $100 to $300, depending on the elegance and location of the establishment. For this price the customer is bathed in a tub, and then rubbed down from head to foot while he lies naked on an inflated rubber mattress. If the client is interested in a more venturesome massage—including extras such as fellatio, cunnilingus, anal stimulation, or sex—it will add anywhere from $300 to $500 to the bill.

All the services offered in the soaplands are camouflaged in the guise of "we are washing the customer." Over the years, establishments throughout the country have contributed their own special brands of sex-massage and intercourse *supesharu* (specials), and have titled them with upbeat suffixes such as play, game, dance, and wash.

Turkish baths, and then later soaplands, were always fiercely competitive among themselves. Each establishment has its *dai* (trainer) whose job it is to keep the soap ladies' technique up to scratch. When a particular place becomes an overnight success, with lines at the door and the parking lot overflowing, rival soaplands instantly send out their *dai* on a spying mission to report on any innovative items on the opponent's menu. The result has been that daringly novel "washes" that had drawn clients to new establishments in places like Kanagawa or Tochigi are now available in all soaplands.

The basic soapland service is *bodii arai* (body wash), in which the soap lady cleans and scrubs the customer, first in the tub then on the mat, until he climaxes. Another basic is *awa odori* (foam dance). In this special wash, the woman pours lotions and creams all over her body and then rubs and "dances" her client to orgasm. In some soaplands this is also known as *shabon dansu* (soap dance). The most popular item on the menu is the *furu kōsu* (full course): a body wash which escalates into a foam dance, followed by an optional body-lick where the client is licked from head to toe, with sexual intercourse as the grand finale.

THE SOAPLAND MENU

ANARU ZEME—Anal Attack
In this type of attack the client's anus is stimulated by massage, fingering, or licking. In some soaplands it can also be used to refer to anal sex, with the customer "attacking" the soap lady.

Other soapland synonyms for anal massage are the fashionable *wan-wan sutairu*, literally the "woof-woof," or what we may call doggie style; *bakon bakon* (bang

bang); and the facetiously circumspect *yoko kara semeru* (conquering from the side).

When a customer wishes to sodomize a soap lady in one of the more luxurious soaplands, the poetic and elegantly evasive term used is *ichi no tani* (the first valley—the second valley being the vagina).

CHIJŌ KIMMU—Ground Servicing
After the customary wash and rub in the bath, the soap lady and her client proceed to the "ground." The girl lies on the mat naked and the customer climbs into a missionary position on top of her.

The other related program is *kūchū kimmu* (aerial servicing), in which the man lies on his back, with the soap lady approaching him from the top.

CHIN ARAI—Penile Wash
Soaplands offer two types of penile wash. In some cases it refers to the soap lady cautiously washing and inspecting the client's organ before she fellates it. In a more luxuriant version the customer relaxes in the bathtub while the woman repeatedly lathers his organ to orgasm.

DABURU—Double
In most soapland services the girl does all the work, while the client lies passively. In *daburu*, from the English word "double," the customer is allowed (for a higher price) to reciprocate the licking while he is being fellated. This is also known as *daburu supesharu* (double special), *daburu supesharu sābisu* (double special service), *daburu gēmu* (double game), and *daburu purē* (double play). Some soaplands also offer their "sixty-nine" programs under the title of *sakasa daburu*

(upside-down double) or *sakasa bodii* (upside-down body), which is short for "upside-down body-wash."

An inspired variation on these games and washes is the *daburu tengu*. *Daburu* refers to the standard sixty-nine position, while *tengu* is a fearsome Japanese forest goblin who has a large red penis-like nose. The client wears the long-nosed *tengu* mask provided by the establishment, and while the soap lady fellates him, he uses it to dildo her.

DAISHARIN ASOBI—Big Wheel Game

The soap lady lies naked on top of her client and stimulates him by slowly moving over him like a wheel, so that he gets to feel and lick the various parts of her body as they cross over his face. A variation of this, also known as *daisharin* (big wheel), is when the client and the girl, one lying on the other, move in opposite directions like two wheels.

Another popular and expensive variation is *tokei asobi* (clock play). The soap lady fellates the supine customer and, without letting go of his organ, crawls clock-wise around his body.

GENBAKU ZEME—Nuclear Bomb Attack

The nuclear bomb attack is administered by soap ladies who specialize in hour-long teasing and tantalizing washes that culminate in explosive orgasms. A similar attack is the *suibaku zeme* (hydrogen bomb attack), in which the client is repeatedly massaged just short of orgasm.

FASHON MASSAJI—Fashion Massage

Fashion massage was invented in the early Turkish baths as a cheaper alternative for clients who prefer to abstain from paying the steeper rates for sex. The original fashion massage was divided into two portions: the regular body-wash, with the topless girl spreading the suds over her client while he sat in the tub, followed by massage on the mat. Instead of finishing off the client with intercourse, the girl would briskly knead and tug at him with her hand.

Fashion massage achieved notoriety by becoming the main service in the booming *herusu* (health) massage parlor industry, where since the seventies it has been served up as fashion massage, or more specifically as *fashon herusu* (fashion health).

HIPPU ARAI—Hip Wash
Hippu, the English word "hip," is a fashionable Japanese sex-trade euphemism for both the backside and the crotch area (it was inspired by *koshi*, its equally obtuse Japanese version). In the hip wash, the naked soap lady lathers her buttocks and the area between her legs and uses them to "wash" her client. In some soaplands this same program is also known as *hippu rōringu* (hip rolling).

JINTAI YOKUJŌ—Human Bathtub
The special feature in the human bathtub service is that the bathtub is missing. In its stead, the soapland provides a "human" tub made of two nude girls— one on each side of the naked client—who wriggle and slide, spreading fragrant foams over his body.

KANZEN PURĒ—Perfect Play
The ordinary soapland customer sits quietly in the tub while the energetic girl gives him a good soaping, and then calmly climbs out, goes to the mat, and,

lying motionlessly face up, waits for his massage. The perfect play was introduced specifically for the more active client. The soap lady lies still and the customer does all of the washing, massaging, stimulating, and licking. The session is then rounded off with inter-course.

KUGURI ARAI—Tunneling Wash

The tunneling wash is one of the most original, if difficult, washes available. The supine and naked soap lady slowly wriggles her way under the prone and naked customer, performing the wash while she is "tunneling" under him. She carefully massages, licks, and bites each of the body parts that she comes in contact with.

An even more venturesome variant of *kuguri arai* is *kuguri tsubo* (tunneling pot). The soap lady uses the same tunneling technique, with the difference that when her *tsubo* (pot) reaches the customer's organ, he may slip it in.

The same service is sometimes billed as *moguri arai* (mole wash) and some soaplands even offer *moguri shaku* (mole blow), along with its expensive variant *moguri namajaku* (mole no-condom blow). The tunnel-ing soap lady crawls and slithers towards the customer's organ, head first. Reaching it, she induces orgasm by fellatio.

KUROSU SUTAIRU—Cross Style

The cross style is an innovative type of wash in which the nude soap lady carefully seats herself on the organ of her supine client. She then massages and stimulates his body, revolving around him until he climaxes.

NAKISEN—Crying Specialty
Naki (crying) is a reference to the gasping or moaning sounds a customer might make while climaxing. In the *nakisen*, also known as *naki senmon* (crying expertise), the soap lady paces herself according to her client's prowess. She will incur the first cry by fellatio, while he is still dressed, the second by climbing into the tub with him, and the third in missionary position on the mat.

NAME ARAI—Lick Wash
After the client has been thoroughly washed in the bathtub the soap lady leads him to the mat, where she gives him a second going over with her tongue. In some soaplands these body licks are also offered as *name sābisu* (licking service).

OTTOSEI ASOBI—Seal Play
Seal play is one of the most expensive soapland services; it can cost thousands of dollars. It borrows its name from the image of a group of seals frolicking in the water. When a customer requests seal play, the management sends him anywhere between four and ten soap ladies to frolic with him. When money is no object, the most luxuriant service is *daimyō asobi* (lord's play) where every free girl on the premises is called in to lick, caress, wash, and rub the lordly client.

PEPĀMINTO SĀBISU—Peppermint Service
Peppermint service, also known in some soaplands as *pepāminto arai* (peppermint wash), is a specialty in which the soap lady either pours peppermint liqueur on her naked client and then licks him all over, or fills her mouth with the liqueur and then tries to spread it

out as evenly as possible from head to foot. A new and humorous name for this wash, inspired by the rise in Japanese earth-awareness, is *ryokuka undō* (parks and gardens movement), a political movement which aims to spread as much green as possible.

Other spirits like whiskey and cognac are also popular as massage lubricants, and are used in services like *sukotchi arai* (scotch wash) and *konnyaku arai* (cognac wash). In some soaplands *sukotchi, konnyaku,* and *pepāminto* are used to refer to oral sex with the masseuse's mouth filled with these stimulants.

SANDOICHI—Sandwich

When a soapland customer requests *sandoichi* (sandwich), *sandoichi sābisu* (sandwich service), or *sandoichi arai* (sandwich wash), it is not out of hunger. These terms refer to the double rub-downs in which the client is expensively sandwiched between two foam-covered naked girls who wriggle and writhe until he has an orgasm. In some soaplands this service is also known as *sandoichi purē* (sandwich play) or just *sando,* for short. Variations are *yoko sando* (horizontal sandwich), with the three lying in a girl-client-girl format, and *tate sando* (standing sandwich), for clients who prefer a vertical wash.

SAZANAMI ODORI—Ripple Dance

After the soap lady has finished washing her client, she dances around him wielding either a beaker of fruit syrup or a cup of cream as he lies dripping and naked on the mat. As the dance climaxes, she pours the liquid in ripples all over his body and then carefully licks him to orgasm. Some soaplands offer a stickier variation called *hachimitsu odori* (honey dance).

SOKUSHAKU—Immediate Blow

When a customer first arrives in the private soap room, many soap ladies, while he is still fully dressed, break the ice with *sokushaku* (immediate fellatio). This is a contraction of *soku* (immediate) and *shakuhachi* (bamboo clarinet), an earthy synonym for oral sex.

Younger clients, and those who can keep up their enthusiasm for the rest of the "full course" session, are encouraged to climax right away.

TAWASHI ARAI—Brush Wash

The brush used in the brush wash is none other than the pubic hair of the soap lady. She applies the foam and works up a lather by slipping and sliding over her customer's naked body. Variations that are available throughout Japan are the *tawashi zeme* (brush assault) and *tawashi odori* (brush dance).

The more fashionable soaplands offer the same type of rub-down under more modern, that is anglicized, names. Some such popular foreign concoctions are *burashi arai* (an amalgam of *burashi*, the Japanese pronunciation of "brush," and *arai*, "wash"), *burashi zeme* (brush assault), *burashi atakku* (brush attack), and *burashi dansu* (brush dance). Another common name for this type of wash is the *junmo zeme* (pure hair assault), where "hair" refers to the girl's pubic area, and "pure" to the fact that she is not wearing panties over them.

In some soaplands the pubic hair program appears more specifically as *pōru burashi purē* (pole brush play). In this case the customer's "pole" is the unique target of the soap lady's "brush."

In the more circumspect soaplands this type of wash is simply known as the *hea arai* (hair wash).

UCHŪ YŪEI—Swimming-in-space

As soaplands frantically searched for new sex ideas, some establishments kept their customer in the bathtub after the initial wash and subjected him to acrobatic intercourse in, on, and under the water. For the swimming-in-space special, the soap lady places the inflatable massage mat over the tub and carefully lies on it. The naked customer, with the help of a little stool, climbs into a perilous missionary position and, "swimming in space," climaxes, tossing and turning with care.

Some other soap ladies do away with the dangerous mat and climb right into the tub while they wash their client. This aquatic missionary position has the scientific title mujūryo yūei (non-gravitational swimming).

In an attempt to expand the possible uses of the wobbly mat, another special, the *uōta-matto odori* (the water-mat dance), was introduced. After his bath is over, the customer is serviced on an air mat full of water.

YAKANHIKŌ—Night Flight

The night flight special begins like any other soapland program with the preliminary bath and full-body rubdown. Once the customer has stepped out of the tub and safely reached the massage mat, the soap lady pulls down the blinds and turns out all the lights (for a touch of atmosphere she might leave a very small red lamp burning on the sideboard). She then carefully feels her way back to the mat, climbs onto the waiting customer, and the night flight begins. She licks, she rubs, and finally she climaxes the client with intercourse.

THE RISE AND FALL OF OGOTO

In the seventies, bigger, better, and cheaper Turkish bathhouses sprang up throughout the provinces of Japan, pushing up the nationwide count from 756 in 1970 to a dizzying 1,575 in 1980. While Tokyo still held the lead with its 257 establishments, new and fashionable provincial sex centers were challenging its supremacy. Kanagawa offered 165 Turkish baths, Hokkaido 85, Chiba 83, Hyōgo 58, Aichi 54, and industrial Saitama, just outside Tokyo, featured unbeatable sale-price body washes at 65 brand new establishments.

This sex-trade expansion catapulted many rural backwater communities into the twentieth century. The overnight appearance of the Turkish baths in some of the most unlikely and remote regions of Japan brought with it real estate speculators, rocketing land prices, the first hotels, shops, supermarkets, restaurants and bars, better roads, and modern housing for the masseuses. Farmers who had barely managed to survive on fields that their families had tilled for generations gaped at the flood of neon, but soon saw the opportunity of a lifetime. Many sold their land at profits that would have been unheard of just months before the baths arrived.

The largest single frenzy of Turkish bath building took place in an unlikely village called Ogoto in the province of Shiga. Before the Bullet Train tracks were laid on its outskirts in 1970, few people had ever been to Ogoto, and before 1960, when the new highways were completed, fewer had even heard of it.

A delicate interplay of circumstances made Ogoto the perfect place for a new sex-trade theme center. It all started rather unexpectedly with the Osaka *Bampaku*, the 1970 Osaka World Fair, when Osaka, literally overrun with tourists for the first time in its history, had to send thousands of visitors out to rural hotels and little inns in the surrounding provinces. Ogoto, everybody suddenly realized, lay within easy distance, and so the first real estate magnates sent out their scouts.

Kaneko Motofumi, a local hotel owner, also amazed at the mass arrival of outsiders, quickly bought up large parcels of land, ostensibly for restaurant development. Close at hand and advising him was Nishiotsutsuji, a gentleman of princely Japanese background who, to the royal family's dismay, had designed the plastic gold-lamé sex-massage tubs that were being used in Turkish baths throughout the country. Buying up land at 7 million yen in 1970, Kaneko Motofumi sold it a year later to *Toruko* builders for 150 million yen.

At the time, the only sex-bathhouse was the Ogoto Sutiimubasu (Ogoto Steambath), a 20-room, 30-girl establishment that catered both to the local farmers and the growing rush of male tourists. On February 6th, 1971, a new bath called Hanakage (Flower Shadow) opened, offering to the crowds of waiting men from Kyoto and Osaka 15 rooms and 20 professional Turkish girls imported from cities throughout Japan. The basic bath fee of ¥500 was a quarter of what the average Tokyo bath charged, and with the bargain full-body massage at ¥3,000 and sex at ¥7,000, this new establishment was headed for success.

February 6th proved to be the most glorious day in

Japanese sex-massage history. Farmers gawked as line upon line of cars and motorcycles inched from Kyoto and Osaka towards the three-story pink and white bath that stood alone among the fields and ditches. Hanakage had expected 50 customers at most, but as customer after customer presented himself, frantic managers started issuing queue numbers and organized the Turkish girls in breakneck shifts. It was only after customer number 300 was led up to his bath by a disheveled Turkish girl who had lost count after her fifteenth that Hanakage locked its doors for the night.

Hanakage was a roaring success. By the end of the week three of its girls escaped and made their way to Tokyo, where they complained to their sex-trade colleagues about the inhumane workload in Ogoto. The Tokyo girls listened in awe. If the runaways lacked the stamina to accommodate 30 men a day—at well over double the average Turkish bath earnings—there were girls who would. Within days, Hanakage was swamped with more eager applicants than it could handle.

The number of customers was also rising steadily, even after the basic bath fee tripled and full-body massage went up to ¥4,000 and sex to ¥10,000. Hanakage had cost 150 million yen to build; within half a year it broke even.

In a few months a rival Turkish bath, Tokyo Toruko, opened, followed closely by Shirayuki (White Snow). The Turkish girls worked their fingers to the bone, but day after day hordes of customers still had to be turned away.

Ogoto was turning into a gold mine, and the sharpest and toughest operators moved in for the kill. First on the scene was the notorious brokeress Madame Yasumoto. Lassoing local farmers, she supervised the selling of their land, acting as intermediary with the out-of-town Turkish magnates. In 1972, the following year, 21 plush new baths opened, followed in 1973 by seven more—each surpassing its predecessor in grandness, garishness, and size. The once quiet, desolate rice fields were now flooded with neon from the baths, bars, novelty stores, supermarkets, and restaurants. Ogoto turned into an all-night sex playground, and soon the farmers were complaining that the harsh neon made their crops fail. More and more of them sold their land and moved out.

The rise of Ogoto was a reflection of the times. The years 1971 and 1972 were to go down in history as the most glorious Turkish years, with a building frenzy that engulfed the entire country. The national Turkish bath count in 1971 was 814. By 1972 it was 1,009, and by 1973 it had reached 1,148. The baths had become such a profitable business that everyone from the Yakuza mob to local politicians, bankers, real estate magnates, and even the police moved in. According to Sanno Shinichi in *Sei no Ōkoku* (The Kingdom of Sex), it was the politicians who benefited the most from the Ogoto baths. He claims that provincial vice-chairman Nagata accepted money from entrepreneurs in exchange for building permits, and that Okumura Etsuzō, vice-governor of Shiga, single-handedly controlled the Ogoto sex-trade boom by deciding who could build what where.

By this time the Nakagawa Yakuza mob had arrived. They dictated policy by controlling the distribution of fuel that kept the baths going and by presiding over deliveries of lunchboxes, flowers, drinks, and most of the essential bath supplies. If an establishment was unwise enough to cross the mob, it could instantly be brought to its knees with a crippling embargo. But Ogoto's sex-trade was pleased with the Yakuza's protection. Criminal elements from Kyoto, Osaka, and Tokyo were kept away, as were the police, and if, as sometimes happened, local hoodlums were misguided enough to run amok in a bath, they were instantly beaten to a pulp. By 1980, a police report established that 13 of Ogoto's 49 Turkish baths were Yakuza-run, but the police did not interfere. When in November of 1982 Sugihara, the ex-chief of police in Osaka, committed suicide, the subsequent inquiry revealed that he and other senior officials had been paid off by mob-run baths throughout the region.

By 1980, Turkish prices had gone up to an average of ¥30,000 for a 40-minute session, of which the girls got to keep from about ¥10,000 to ¥15,000. In a busy bath a girl could earn in a day what a blue collar worker earned in a month. To apply for a job as a Turkish girl at an Ogoto bath, the applicant would walk up Champs Elysses Street with two photographs of herself in her hand and knock at the door of the Shigaken Tokushu Yokujo Kyōkai (Shiga Special Bath Association). After she registered, one of the photographs would be filed and the other sent to police headquarters. Besides welcoming new Turkish girls, one of the Special Bath Association's main jobs was to ensure optimum public relations. The office walls were cluttered with official commendations, thank-yous from VIPs, and certificates and trophies for charity work. Tamori Yoshiro, the idealistic director of the association, regularly praised his Turkish girls;

he even went so far as to gather *haiku* for a Turkish girl poetry book.

According to Tamori, the Turkish boom did more than just bring prosperity and happiness to Ogoto; it helped calm the libido of many an excitable local man. In 1970, before Ogoto's transformation, Tamori argued, there were 57 reported rapes and no less than 51 indecent exposures. After Hanakage opened its doors in 1971, only 38 women were raped and 29 sexually harassed, and by the time Tokyo Toruko and Shirayuki were in full swing the following year, rapes were down to 31 and sexual assaults to 21. By the time Ogoto had reached its peak in 1979, with 49 baths, only seven women were raped.

By the early eighties, Ogoto's novelty was paling and the Turkish boom ground to a halt. The 49 bath establishments fought alongside the rest of Japan's faltering massage-trade businesses to keep customers interested, some by dropping their prices drastically, others by tuning their Turkish girls' technique to an ever-finer pitch, but in spite of their efforts the patrons' attention was wandering. In July, 1978, JANI (Johnny), Japan's first *nopan kissa* (no-panty coffee shop) had opened in Kyoto, starting a new rage that engulfed the nation. Ogoto's customers flocked in droves to these new cheap establishments to peek up waitresses' skirts for a few hundred yen. Soon even more dangerous competitors opened shop: "pink" cabarets, followed closely by "pink" salons, saunas, massage-rooms, and bars where orgasms were dealt out not only in titillating new settings, but at a fraction of the Turkish cost.

Then the mid-eighties brought the new fiercer public-morality laws and the first Ogoto baths closed.

OGOTO—1993

Two decades after Ogoto saw its first bath mushroom in a field, its face is once again changing. The traffic jams, the eager crowds, the mini-skirted soap ladies have for the most part moved on. The streets are empty and the parking lots dark. Thirty-nine soaplands remain, but most are not doing too well.

The only Ogoto soaplands still in full swing are establishments with a gimmick. A successful one is Fushigi no Kuni no Arisu (Alice in Wonderland), whose claim to distinction is that it is the cheapest soapland in Japan. From 9 a.m. to 6 p.m. a wash is priced at $80 (prime-time washes go for $90), with the added incentive that full refunds are given to clients who climax more than three times. Elegance is not Alice in Wonderland's forte. One has to pay on entering, wait in a no-frills waiting room, and the washes last only 30 minutes. But Alice has tried to make up for her roughness by undergoing a top-to-bottom renovation in 1992 and hiring attractive, hard-working girls who can handle a quick turnover.

At the other end of the scale is Kurosu (Cross), a soapland that keeps customers coming by being among the most expensive in Japan. It offers quality, style, and elegance, starting at $550. The waiting room is tastefully decorated, a piano provides refined background music, the elevator to the room is private, and the soap ladies could be models. Kurosu fosters the illusion that the client is visiting his high-class mistress in her apartment and that she, pleased to see him, bathes and massages him to orgasm.

3 • THE HEALTH BOOM

While the Turkish bathhouses of the seventies were expanding and upgrading their massage menus, charging up to $400 and $500 for all-out intercourse, another branch of the sex industry began to muscle in on their territory, offering the more frugal customer discount orgasms at $30 and $40. These parlors started appearing in all the old Turkish neighborhoods, and came to be known as *herusu* (health) from the "fashion health" services that they offered.

The health girls in these establishments would massage, lick, penetrate with and be penetrated by rubber batons and vibrators, but they escaped the anti-prostitution squad by forbidding customers what the police label *seiki no ketsugyō* (the connecting of sex organs).

As the early *herusu* proprietors quickly realized, the kinkiest services fell outside the boundaries of "connecting of the sex organs." The basic fashion health massage, for instance (also known in health circles as *yubi man*, "finger cunt") is perfectly legal. The health girl helps her client undress, shows him to the shower, and joins him there for a *chin arai* (penile wash), which gives her the opportunity for a quick health inspection. If he passes the test she leads him to a mat, where for 15 or 20 minutes she will palpate him to orgasm. In a no-frills *herusu* like Gypsy Queen in

Kyoto, or Yancha Hime (Naughty Princess) in the Sakae District of Nagoya City, this basic service is available for about $45, while clients who are willing to brave the earthiness of Sexy Mates in Fukuoka City's Nakasu District can come away for as little as $25.

In general, during these *regurā* (regular) services the health girl remains topless but pantied. In some *herusu*, like Osaka's Bunny, if a small tip is added to the $75 fee the panties come off, whereas in other more expensive Tokyo places like New York in the Shibuya District and Orange Box in Shimbashi, the girls not only take their panties off but hand them out as gifts on festive occasions.

Another fashion health option which involves no illegal connecting of the organs is "lip service," the professional word for fellatio. Even in the most humble *herusu* this is the deluxe special, and the masseuse will spend between 20 and 30 minutes on her client. If one requests this service in an establishment where there is no shower, the health girl appears with a batch of hot and steamy *oshibori* towels, of the kind that are offered to diners in Japanese restaurants. She unzips the client, sprays him with disinfectant, gives him a good scrubbing with one *oshibori* after another, and, saving a towel for the end, approaches him with her mouth.

With the marginal increase of AIDS awareness in Japan in the nineties, most modern-minded places now offer "skin-lip service"—fellatio with a condom. In many of the better *herusu*, however, customers get to remove their condoms in order to perform the pricey and increasingly fashionable *ganmen hassha* (face ejaculation). Circus Lady, for instance, a *herusu* in the Kita District in Osaka, dresses up its girls as executive secretaries and then offers *sekuhara purē* (sexual harassment play). The more you pay the more you can harass. The basic services are the *salariiman* (office worker) and the *kachō sābisu* (section chief service) in which the client can touch his assigned secretary's breasts, whisper coarse epithets in her ear, and demand that she remove her panties and fondle him to orgasm. In the more sophisticated $130 *shachō supesharu* (company president special), the harasser can order his secretary to undress and engage for 40 minutes in *tamakorogashi* (ball licking) and sixty-nine. The most expensive sexual harassment available at Circus Lady is the *kaichō supesharu* (company chairman special). For $160, it is up to the client if he wants to wear a condom, and at the end of his allotted 40 minutes he is allowed to ejaculate, uttering a string of obscenities, over his secretary's face.

The only type of actual sex that a *herusu* will offer on its massage menu is anal intercourse. Technically this does not involve the proscribed "connecting of the sex organs" that could expose the girls to the danger of raids, for although according to Japanese law the penis is sexual, the anus is not. *Herusu* that offer this service have signs saying "Our girls are aggressive," and even "Ask for Hitomi, she likes it from behind." The man at the door cautions that all "anal attacks" must be executed with a condom.

Throughout the early eighties the *herusu* industry grew rapidly. It borrowed from its rival bathhouses many of the services like *paizuri* (breast-urbation) and *sōname* (full-body licks) and even adopted the characteristic massage mats. Some *herusu*, like the Mirāshon in Nagoya City, went so far as to install the pervert chairs that were the bathhouse rage in the late seventies. In two ways, however, the *herusu* steered clear from the Turkish baths. It refused to install tubs, and it refused to offer sex. This was what saved the *herusu* industry in 1985 when the *Shinfūei Hō*, the New Sex Business Law, crashed down on the bathhouse industry, dealing it what many thought at the time a death blow. While the bathhouses were being raided constantly, their closed-door massages declared illegal, their requests for building permits and operating licenses delayed or turned down, the *herusu* really came into their own.

By the late eighties the bathhouses, which by then had been re-baptized from *Toruko* to soaplands, were visibly losing popularity. After three decades the tired clientele was beginning to look elsewhere for stimulation. Many felt that after years of training, the soap ladies had lost their spontaneity and turned into robotic specialists. Nervously, the soaplands continued to upgrade their services, but as the nineties approached what the public really wanted was for the charming and innocent high school girl-next-door to service them. The *herusu* industry obliged. A health girl did not have to be sophisticated to get hired; as the recruiting ads in the local newspapers often point out, "Even provincials with very strong dialects will be considered—bright smile a must."

It was, however, not so much hapless provincials who applied at the *herusu* but college students and secretaries. These were the affluent eighties, with their demand for fast cars, expensive restaurants, and brand name clothing and accessories. Unfashionable girls at fashionable universities would find themselves snubbed by all the tennis, golf, and literary

clubs that a girl had to belong to in order to get on in academia. With just a few quick hours of work a day an eager young girl could live in the manner to which everyone was becoming accustomed.

As the health girls became more scintillating, even more soapland clients left the company of the experienced soap ladies for the simpler services. Word got round that you could talk to health girls, that you could develop a relationship with them if you came often enough. By 1990 the *shirōto būmu* (amateur boom) was in full swing. High school uniforms, bunny outfits, and baby-doll lingerie was in, and even veteran soap ladies and the older health girls obliged. Management was faced with the problem of offering workers who were innocent enough to bring the customer in off the street but knowledgeable enough to keep him from demanding his money back.

The interior decoration of most *herusu* is stark, dusty, and geared towards efficiency. A pungent smell of cigarette smoke and disinfectant hangs in the air. As one enters the *machiai shitsu* (meeting room), a young man who is referred to in the *herusu* world as the "waiter" rattles off the price list and raves about a particularly talented and innocent health girl. The sophisticated customer, however, ignores his advice. He knows that he might be exposing himself to what the sex trade calls *san-bii kiken* (3-B danger), where the uninspected girl might well turn out to be *busu* (ugly), *baba* (an old bitch), and *botakuri* (a rip-off). For a mere $10 to $15 extra, the customer can relax and make his choice from the polaroids that are pinned up on a plywood board whenever the girls are between stints. Some of the newer *herusu* have a VCR next to the drink machine, and the girls introduce themselves in short interviews on tape and discuss the types of service they offer. An increasing number of *herusu*, like Tokyo's New York II in the Ebisu area and the American Blue in Meguro, divide their waiting rooms with a two-way mirror. The girls are parked on one side and read, watch television, or throw a few yen into the drink machine, while the customer, hidden from view on the other side, discreetly makes his choice.

The health girl who is selected leads her customer down the corridor to her minuscule "fashion room." There is barely enough space for the bed and the heap of stuffed animals that are meant to accentuate her youth and innocence. In most of the $40 and $50 places the masseuse gets right down to business, as an exceedingly quick turnover is of paramount importance. Other places, like Osaka's Angel Kiss with its $90 specials, allow clients to sit on the side of the bed for a few minutes, make small talk, and sip on a complimentary beer.

By early 1992 the *herusu* boom was reaching its climax. As Fukasawa Kaoru pointed out in an article in the magazine *Marco Polo*, there were over 90 establishments in Tokyo alone. The competition was mounting, and the *herusu* were forced to change, expand, and adapt as the Turkish baths had done two decades earlier. To do well each place had to develop special gimmicks. Some *herusu*, like the Shimbashi Girl School in Tokyo, with its collection of giggly and pigtailed masseuses, invested in a brazen aura of innocence. As the neon billboard at the entrance proclaims, "tuition" is either $80 or $90, depending on the "class" one wishes to attend. Other *herusu*, like Osaka's brash Girls 69, renounced any possible claim to virtue by advertising their $100 eponymous house-special in red lights. The Pink Palace in Osaka and the Tsubasa (Wings) in Nagoya revolutionized the *herusu* concept by introducing *gyaku-herusu* (inverted health) and W-Touch (pronounced *daburuyū-tachi*), short for "woman touch." In both cases the health girl lies motionless and naked on the mat, while the customer, for 20 minutes, is allowed to become a health boy and vigorously massage away. The Mascot in the Kita District in Osaka went off at an even more profitable tangent introducing the immensely popular *hitozuma kōsu* (housewife course) with its prized collection of real-life married matrons.

The K-Club, which opened in the early nineties near Tenman Station in Osaka, set itself apart by selling its own unique "boss special." The health girl appears in the playroom wearing a dainty thong. She places by her mattress a white kitchen-timer which she sets to 20 minutes and, spraying the naked customer with disinfectant, she licks him to orgasm before the time is up. When the timer goes off, she dries him and leaves so that the next girl can take her post. She in turn winds up her own white timer, sprays the man with disinfectant and quickly tries to revivify him for a second 20-minute stint. The price is $150.

Other *herusu* have continued thriving by keeping their "play time" as cheap as possible and by constantly offering their clients new health girls and new massage games. One of the more modest places in the Kita District in Osaka is the older but still wildly successful Ichigo Hausu (Strawberry House). Its claim to fame is that not only can it satisfy anyone in under 15 minutes, but that over the years it has managed to keep going a constant stream of eccentric massages, like the *otete supesharu* (patticake-patticake special) and the famous crowd-pleaser *onanii mekakushi purē* (blindfolded masturbation play).

Some of the less imaginative herusu, like the Dragon Ball in Osaka's Kita district, managed to squeeze in more guests by drastically shortening their "play time," guaranteeing an orgasm in 15 minutes or less for under $30. Other places went the opposite direction. The Vitamin C in the Nogizaka District in Tokyo and the Mushroom in Roppongi, both owned by the same family, offer for $135 their elegant services in rooms equipped with plants, landscape paintings, and soft music droning over the loudspeaker. San-Jū Ro (Thirty Roads) and Alice went even further and became famous for being more expensive than many of the top soapland bathhouses. Don Juan, which opened in Tokyo's Shinjuku District, outdid all the others in quality and style. It attracted the richest clientele by offering triple-X video stars, and gained notoriety as the single most expensive herusu in all of Japan. A basic 90-minute special started at $600 and a VIP program went for well over $1,000.

THE HEALTH MENU

A-ZEME—A-attack

Most *herusu* offer a selection of "A" or "anal" attacks. In the standard "A" service the health girl approaches the client from behind with a finger or a vibrator while she is massaging him with her free hand from the front. (In some programs it is the client who does the fingering.)

In a creative variation known as *A-zeme pāru* (A-attack pearl), the woman threads a long string of delicate pearls into the customer's anus and then, while she is fellating him, yanks at the string, making the pearls bob out one by one.

The rougher *herusu* also offer an expensive *A-zeme-F*. The "F" in this case stands for "fuck," the implication being that the client may sodomize the health girl.

BODII TACHI—Body Touch
The health girl removes her massage apron and bra, applies fragrant lotion to her chest, and lying down on the naked customer begins touching him with her body from head to foot.

CHOTTO DAKE YO—Just For a Bit
After a health girl has massaged and fellated her client she may stray, and for an extra charge, let him slip his penis into her vagina—just for a bit. Herusu establishments strongly frown on this practice, for if a woman's room happens to be raided by the police during one of her *chotto dake yo*, fines, arrests, and crippling court cases follow.

In some *herusu* these hurried and illegal bouts of intercourse are also known as *chonnoma* (quickie), a term borrowed from the street corners, where it refers to a prostitute's short $100 stint.

EREGANSU MASSAJI—Elegance Massage
This is a fashionable reference to the fundamental service available in all *herusu*. Elegantly, the woman works her way up to the customer's organ which she then robustly massages. Many *herusu* refer to this as their *bijinesu kōsu* (business course) the idea being that it is suitable for busy professionals on a coffee break.

This service is also less elegantly referred to as *yubi pisuton* (finger piston).

GANMEN HASSHA—Facial Blast
The facial blast is part of the uncondomed fellatio program. The customer, approaching orgasm, utters the formula, "Ikisō, ikisō"—"I think I'm coming, I think I'm coming." At this the health girl quickly

snatches his organ out of her mouth and points it towards her face.

In some *herusu* this practice is referred to as *gansha* (face shot). If, however, the health girl should be too late, this same service changes into *kōnai hassha* (mouth blast). With the growing fear of AIDS, most urban *herusu* discourage mouth blasts and present facial ejaculation as a titillatingly sadistic alternative. As the customer climaxes over the health girl's face she writhes, humiliated and in anguish, moaning, "Iya, iya, dame"—"No, no, you shouldn't."

Some of the more prudent *herusu* have recently introduced *gomu kōnai hassha* (condom mouth-blast).

KANCHŌ PURĒ—Enema Play

Enema enthusiasts who enjoy giving or receiving enemas during sex, or as a substitute for it, are known in Japanese sex-trade circles as *kanchō-ma* (enema fiends). Their enemas are known as *ero-kanchō* (erotic enemas) or *sekkusu kanchō* (sex enemas), and are offered at some of the more progressive soaplands and *herusu*.

KAOMISE KISSU—Face-showing Kiss

The modern *herusu* customer is wary of handing over his hard-earned yen at the reception desk unless he has personally looked over all the available women. For this inspection some places installed expensive two-way mirrors, others went for the cheaper polaroid billboard. In February of 1993, a Tokyo *herusu* called Fantasy launched a new trend know as the face-showing kiss. The customer pays at the reception and is immediately led into a private room where he sits on the bed and waits. The door opens, a health girl rushes in, kisses him, and rushes out. A few minutes later another girl appears, pecks him on the cheek, and bolts out again.

After the fourth girl leaves, a waiter enters the room, bows, and asks the customer to decide which girl he would like for the one-hour, $100 program.

KOKKU SAKKINGU—Cocksucking

A direct borrowing from American slang, this expression takes on new meanings in Japanese. As a special service the health girl, before she fellates a customer, might use ketchup or teriyaki sauce as a tangy lubricant.

KUNI SĀBISU—"Cunni" Service

"Cunni" is a discreet cropping of the word cunnilingus. In this service the health girl lies completely still while the customer takes over. In some *herusu*, such as the New York in Shibuya, *kuni sābisu* refers specifically to a no-panty sixty-nine position; while the health girl works on the client, he may reciprocate.

NIRINSHA—Two-Wheeler

If the adventurous customer is prepared to pay double, many *herusu* will offer him the option of playing "bicycle" with not one woman, but two. The two health girls, one on each end, are the wheels. This program appears on many *herusu* menus as *toripuru purē* (triple play), an expression borrowed from the soapland competition, and also, more cryptically, as *san-pii* (3-P), short for "3 persons." A parlor in Sapporo called Pretty Girl is notorious for its special 3-P program, in which the third person is an inflatable doll, naked but for its expensive imported panties.

A common variation of 3-P is *san-pii rezu* (3 persons lesbian). Two health girls appear arm in arm, undress each other in front of the customer, and, for the first half of the session, roll about on the massage mat while he watches. In the second half, the client undresses and joins the women.

The customer with even more yen to spend can opt for the *sanrinsha* (three-wheeler), where he gets three women. This is also offered by some of the more exclusive places as *toroika* (troika).

SEKAI ISSHŪ—Globe-Trotting

The globe in this case is the customer's body, and the trotting is done by the health girl's tongue. After the customer has showered, she picks an extremity and starts licking towards his organ, which she keeps missing until the very last moment. Another ebullient name for this same service is *sōname* (total victory). It is written with the characters *sō* (complete) and *name* (lick).

In the safe-sex-conscious nineties, some health girls abstain from fellatio and perform the full-body licks while massaging the client's organ. Others, on reaching the organ, excuse themselves, reach over for the condom, and finish the client off with *fera-kabuse* (covered fellatio). Many women, however, believe that these various forms of *name ensō* (lick performance) are AIDS-safe as long as they gargle vigorously after the client leaves.

SHAKUHACHI—Bamboo Flute

This traditional instrument, wooden and clarinet-like in shape, has become the single most popular Japanese sex-trade word for fellatio. Outside some of the bolder *herusu*, signs with blinking red lights announce: "Shakuhachi—¥12,000" or "Akiko's shakuhachi #1." In many *herusu*, fellatio also appears on the menu as the more polite *oshaku* ("o" being an elegant particle often translated into English as "honorable," and *shaku* the truncated version of *shakuhachi*).

In the nineties, as more *herusu* have turned to fellatio, *shakuhachi* comes in many packages.

The rhyming *bakku-shakku* (back flute) for instance, requires that the customer lie on his stomach while the health girl, forcefully slithering on her back, squeezes her way under his thighs. She finally performs the fellatio with the full weight of his body on her face.

With the AIDS scare came *gomu-shaku* (rubber flute); the health girl slips a condom over the customer's organ before approaching it. By extension, *nama-jaku* (raw flute) without the complication of condoms, has been elevated, both in the soaplands and the *herusu* to the rank of an expensive delicacy. In its deluxe variation, known as *kanzen nama-jaku* (total raw-flute), the client is even permitted to climax in the health girl's mouth.

Another product of AIDS consciousness is *bōru-jaku* (combining the English "balls" with *shaku*) and its all-Japanese version *tama-jaku* (*tama*, "balls"). The health girl sucks the client's testicles while she works his organ with her hand.

Many contemporary *herusu* now also offer *te-shaku* (hand flute). The health girl rubs lotion into her palms, kneels beside her client who is lying naked on his back, and begins kneading him to orgasm. The client closes his eyes and fantasizes that it is her mouth and not her hand that is stimulating him.

A related euphemism popular in the *herusu* world is the *yokobue* (cross flute). While the *shakuhachi* enters the mouth of the player, the *yokobue* player merely places his lips on the instrument's hole. *Yokobue purē* (side-flute play) in a *herusu* entails the customer cunnilinging the health girl.

SHINGURU—Single

In the older, no-frills *herusu*, single refers to massage which aims to climax clients in the shortest possible time. The health girl whips off her bra, drags down her client's pants, and aspires to rub him to orgasm in just under ten minutes. Some *herusu* also bill this service as *onanisuto supesharu* (onanist special).

In the nineties, as fellatio has become more of a staple in the *herusu* industry, *shinguru* can refer to a hurried and unadorned oral session.

SUMATA—Between the Thighs

This is the closest that a law-abiding health girl comes to allowing the illegal "connecting of the sex organs." She lies on her back, smears lotion on her upper thighs, and clasps the customer, who lies down on top of her, firmly between her legs. In some *herusu* this is offered as *porujime sābisu* (pole-clenching service).

WAKAME SHIGEKI—Seaweed Stimulation

Desperately seeking innovative body rubs, the *herusu* industry has recently revived this seaweed special, which had become the rage in the Turkish baths of the seventies. The health girl is supplied with buckets of slithery boiled seaweed, which she trowels onto her body. The naked client climbs onto her, and climaxes by wriggling and sliding over the soggy green mush.

YUBIHAWASE—Finger Crawl

The health girl's fingers crawl over the customer's body. She repeatedly brushes against, but misses, his organ until it's *panchi taimu* (punch time), the crucial final five minutes of the service. At this point she zeros in and frenetically manipulates away. If the customer fails to climax, the management will have to refund his money.

ZENRĀ SĀBISU—Stark-Naked Service

In this case, not only the customer is *zenrā* (stark naked), but so is the health girl. Many establishments have stuck to the original 1970s' *herusu* credo, which dictated that the women could work topless but would have to remain safely pantied. (This way, if the police launched a surprise anti-prostitution raid, no one could be dragged off in handcuffs.) Throughout the eighties and nineties, however, the more competitive and hard-core among the *herusu* began undressing their women completely. These naked massages are also offered under the English title *ōru nūdo* (all nude).

* * *

In the summer of 1992 the Japanese economy slid into a surprise recession. There was a wave of new competition as many of the shoddier soaplands, constantly harassed by the police and now abandoned by their clients, transformed themselves into cheaper *herusu* in an attempt to survive. They changed their names and removed sex from their menus, but otherwise left their decor and private rooms with tubs and mats intact. Some places, like the Nyū Gurando (New Grand) in Tokyo's Kabukichō, went both ways. From

8 a.m. to 1 p.m. it's health time, with $90 massage packages custom-made for harried businessmen on coffee breaks, while in the long quiet hours of the afternoon the Nyū Gurando switches back to its old $220 soapland ways.

Many provincial *herusu* found themselves badgered into becoming semi-soaplands. The younger generation was eager for the modern and cheaper health massages, but hordes of older clients demanded their baths and *honban* (performance) that invariably followed. One such staunch anti-*herusu* outpost was the Sakae District in Chiba, which by the early eighties was teeming with 85 soaplands but did not have a single *herusu*. Even as the panic over the 1992 recession grew stronger, the old soaplanders stuck to their massage mats and refused to consider the cheaper and more fashionable alternatives. The first *herusu* to dare open shop in Chiba was the Crystal. With its vibrant decor and its $120 specials, the enthusiastic crowd at first mistook it for some kind of kinky but cheap soapland. Enthusiasm, however, quickly turned to outrage when men realized sex was denied them. Sales plummeted, and fearing bankruptcy the owners quickly ordered a tub for every room and charged $50 extra for sex.

By the autumn of 1992 the most expensive soaplands and the cheapest were still doing remarkably well, but many "middle-class" establishments in the $250 range hit the skids, and soap ladies desperate for work started knocking on *herusu* doors. The average age in the *herusu* started rising as the tough new girls, often in their late twenties and early thirties, mingled with the college-age health girls. Customers left, complaining that the *herusu* were losing their simplicity and that their services smacked increasingly of soapland.

The new girls were not satisfied either. They complained to their *herusu* managers that the policy of inducing orgasm by fellatio was exceptionally strenuous and undignified, especially if a successful girl's daily quota was seven to nine customers. Straightforward sex, they argued, even if illegal, was the least taxing way of prompting orgasms. Many *herusu* relented. They were not about to put up neon signs (as some soaplands were known to do) advertising their lax policies, but left it up to the health girls to decide if they liked their customers enough to sleep with them.

4 • EROGENOUS ZONE PARLORS

Just as the *herusu* frenzy was reaching its peak late in 1991, the new *seikan massaji*—the erogenous massage parlors—arrived as serious competitors. The *herusu*'s historic mark had been that it simplified the intricate, costly, and time-consuming washes of the soapland bathhouses and offered its customers clean, quick, and cheap fixes. Shrewd sex-traders, however, were quick to predict that the *herusu* concept was not substantial enough to keep the crowds captivated for long.

The *herusu* industry had its shortcomings. A major complaint was that the health girls were no longer as innocent or amateurish as fashion demanded. Furthermore, with the growing fear of AIDS, clients began wondering whether the erotic "health" services were as safe as they should be. Fellatio had become the staple offering, and anxious men stopped the girls at *tamakorogashi* (testicle licking) while massaging themselves to orgasm.

The time had come to launch a new type of sex parlor, sophisticated but simple, with an upbeat clinical name like *seikan* (sexual sensitizing), also known more delicately in some neighborhoods as *mensu esute* (men's beauty parlors). There was to be no intercourse, and in the original parlors no fellatio, just the house specialty: hard driving *senritsuzen zeme* (prostate gland attacks) in the form of anal massage administered while rubbing clients' organs.

The magnates built their *seikan* parlors similar enough to the *herusu* to make customers feel at home, but different enough to bring them racing in. Many of Osaka's parlors presented themselves (depending on the client's interests) as *herusu* to some and as *seikan* to others. The Mascot, for instance, in the Kita District catered to its more frugal clients with a discounted *herusu* option at $80, while charging $120 for its *seikan* services, which were becoming ever more popular. Another typical Osaka parlor, the Reijō (Young Lady), which opened right across from the train station in Jūsō, presented itself to its public as a *seikan-herusu*. It managed to snatch up kinkier clients from the many local S&M clubs by adding a $250 "deluxe" sado-service to its roster.

The *seikan* magnates helped their new clubs by roping in the media, getting the *seikan* girls onto talk shows, "what's-new-on-the-streets specials," and launching discussions on late-night TV shows. Magazine reporters spent their time parlor-hopping, sampling new prostate specials from Tokyo to Osaka, analyzing, comparing, and awarding stars. By mid-1992 *seikan* was in full swing.

The layout of the new parlors was similar to the *herusu*. Clients walk into what is usually a dusty reception room filled with cigarette smoke, where they can discuss prices and prostate-massage options with the "waiter." The *seikan*, like its sister-parlor the *herusu*, has adopted the *shimeiryō* system in which for an extra $10 to $15 clients can choose a specific girl. Simple decor and a quick turnover are an important element in keeping prices competitive, so the faded sofas in the waiting room are usually threadbare, the plastic chairs uncomfortable, the well-leafed magazines old, and the ashtrays full of cigarette butts. As the client is led down a musty corridor he could well be walking through a *herusu*. The massage room is also familiar in that it is very small, unaired and has an unmistakable stench strongly laced with perfume. The customer undresses, and the girl prepares her *yubisakku* (finger sack) which she nimbly slips over her middle finger. She lays out some wet towels, wipes the client meticulously, and then, rolling him onto his stomach, pours lotion between his legs, jabbing away gently with her *yubisakku*. As she gains momentum and the client becomes more excited, the *seikan* girl will turn him onto his back. Facing him, she slides her thighs under his buttocks to prop him up, and then executes the final frontal and posterior stimulation in what is known in the trade as *panchi taimu* (punch time), the frenetic five minutes at the end of the service dedicated to guaranteeing an orgasm.

Seikan girls usually wear trendy lingerie unless the customer specifically asks for the more expensive *ōru nūdo* (all nude). In Tokyo, a *seikan* parlor in Roppongi even called itself T-Bakku (T-back) from the aerobics-type thong that became a nationwide success with young and old when Japan's 1992 porn-superstar, Iijima Ai, came out with her triple-X video "T-back Queen." The *seikan* girls of the T-Bakku parlor work on their clients thonged and topless, and distinguish themselves from other Roppongi District professionals by what the parlor calls *kyonyū chinbasami* (large-chest penile-clenching), in which the girl jiggles the customer to orgasm with her breasts, while she fingers him with her free hand.

The *seikan* parlors like the *herusu* clubs were quick in developing their own distinctive characteristics. The Orange Club in the Shinjuku District in Tokyo concocted an especially explosive 90-minute "powder massage" which it dealt out at $220 a shot. Another Tokyo *seikan* parlor, one of the most renowned in the Gotanda District, the Ni-jū-yon Kin Gorudo (24-Karat Gold), went so far as to invent its own gold-colored lotion. Parlor policy dictates that the girls, as a special erotic effect, smack their lips and slurp loudly as they massage their clients in the glittering substance.

By 1993 most *seikan* parlors had decided that business came first and principles second. The recession seemed to be gaining momentum but the *seikan* boom was not. More men had to be wrenched away from the *herusu* and the only way to do that was to drop the original no-fellatio policy which would inevitably bring in clientele addicted to "lip service." The ploy worked, and all over Japan, the new parlors proudly instituted *rippu seikan* (lip sensitizing), with masseuses who nimbly fingered away while they climaxed the client with "mouth service." The *herusu* industry was outraged. Quick to retaliate, it heisted its rival's *esute* or "beauty" massage, and lured back clients who had acquired a taste for anal stimulation. Expensive newspaper ads pointed out that health girls were trained in *baibu sonyū* (vibrator assaults) which surely were more potent than anything a *seikan* girl with a finger sack could do. A boisterous tug-of-war started, with parlors grabbing at each other's clients and pirating each other's specialties, and out of the skirmish a new successful breed of *seikan* emerged, elegantly skimming together the best of both worlds.

Parlors like the Daiamondo Biryō (Diamond Villa) in Tokyo's Ikebukuro District, forged best-selling stunts like *zenritsusen oiru massaji* (prostate oil massage) and the $150 *zenshin rippu sābisu* (full-body lip service), and the deluxe $170 *zenshin A-rippu kōsu* (full-body A-lip course) in which the "A" stands for "anal." Right next door, the Goruden Biryō (Golden Villa) catered to a tougher and richer client who was prepared to pay $250 dollars and up for a *peropero* (quiver-all-over) special. The *seikan* girl begins with the low-key kneading and the penetrative jabs available at all *seikan* parlors. She is naked except for a very modest apron. Twenty minutes into the *peropero* massage, her apron, without warning, drops off and she lunges onto the customer, who is lying on his back at this point, and slides up and down in a *bodii arai* (body wash), a technique borrowed from the soaplands. The next surprise is known as *oppai seikan* (breast sensitizing), in which the nipple replaces the usual sack-covered middle finger, followed by a final climactic *A-name* (anal lick).

In the meantime, the S&M boom was gaining momentum, and *seikan* customers increasingly requested to be manhandled. Osaka had already experimented successfully with its first S&M erogenous massage parlors, and soon Tokyo followed suit. Cappuccino in the Shinjuku District went part of the way with its clients' wishes, adapting itself to placate the masochists with *sofuto emu-purē* (soft M-play) but drawing the line when it came to sadism. The Aoi Gensō (Blue Fantasy) added to its massages the $180 *kōsoku emu-esute sābisu* (restricted M-beauty service), in which clients are first tied up and then molested by the masseuses penetrating fingers.

One of the first places to seriously fuse the art of erogenous massage with that of sadomasochism was the Rankōporēshon (its vivacious name inspired by a fusion of *ranko*, "gang-bang" and "corporation") a *seikan* parlor in Tokyo, near the train station in Ikebukuro. The haughty erogenous princess appears in extravagant leather lingerie and must at all times be addressed as *ohime-sama* (oh princess most grand). Her first demand is that the filthy client grovel off into the topnotch bathroom for a shower. When he re-emerges, a demure towel around his waist, the *seikan* special begins, with the slight twist, however, that he is the one who has to perform it on himself. "Turn your back to me! Whip it out! Stimulate it!" she barks at him. "Careful, I'm watching you in the mirror!... Now, slip your finger in, yes, down there!" As the client has to pay $150 for an hour of erogenous humiliation, the haughty princess finally relents and, coming down from her elevated pedestal, personally fingers him to orgasm.

THE SEIKAN MENU

ANARU ZEME—Anal Attack

The anal attacks in the *seikan* parlors have been specifically set up to stimulate the customer's *senritsuzen*, his prostate gland. While the rivaling soaplands and *herusu* offer their own anal attacks, these pale beside the deep and intense manipulation offered by the trained *seikan* specialists.

In some parlors anal service is also known as *ei-tachi* (a-touch) and *ei-kankaku* (a-sensitizing—the discreet "a" in both cases being short for anus). Other places, however, prefer exotically scientific names such as *senritsuzen shigoki* (prostate stimulation), *senritsuzen oiru* (prostate oil, implying that massage oil is used as a soothing lubricant), and even *senritsuzen baibu* (prostate vibe), in which electric vibrators are used.

In the most expensive *seikan* parlors, lengthy and delicate penetration is circumspectly offered as *komon-sama sābisu* (lord anus service).

ANARU-SHŪCHU RIPPU—Anal-Centralization Lip

This impressive-sounding program is popular in tougher urban parlors like Tokyo's Daiamondo Biryō (Diamond Villa). It comes in two versions. The *seikan* girl will either massage the client's prostate gland while she applies her lip to his penis, or in the more devil-may-care parlors actually centralize her lips on his posterior. Some *seikan* parlors offer this same service as *anaringusu* (analingus).

FINGA PURĒ—Finger Play

Finger play is the type of service in which the *seikan* girl works her way as tantalizingly as possible over her customer's body until she reaches his organ, which she then deftly manipulates to orgasm. The same type of service is also known as *fingaringu* (fingering) and *finga sābisu* (finger service), both of which also involve the lubricated stimulation of the customer's anus.

In a variation sometimes known as *gyaku finga purē* (inverted finger play), the *seikan* girl lies still on the mat while her customer is allowed to stimulate her.

In cases where the client wishes his organ to be the sole focus of a massage, *seikan* parlors offer what is known as *hando pompu sābisu* (hand pump service).

HANE NO HANA—Feather Flower
The client takes his shower and lies down on the mat for his prostate stimulation. After the *seikan* girl has spent the first half of the service rubbing and jabbing at the gland, she removes her finger sack and reaches to the sideboard for a colorful flower-like feather duster. The client falls exhausted on his back while the woman dusts and tickles him to orgasm. In parlors where a single feather is used, this service is known as *umō zeme* (plume attack).

HERUPU—Help
When the client asks for help in a *seikan* parlor, the management sends him two women: a senior *seikan* girl with an assistant who helps her work on him. While the senior girl dispenses an anal massage, the junior girl might work on the customer's neck, his lower back, or even his organ. Some parlors use the "help special" as a handy and profitable way of training new, inexperienced women. In soapland bathhouses, such as the Taipei in Tokyo's old Yoshiwara district, help also comes in the form of two women, with the difference however, that these work as equals, without one ordering the other around.

HŌZURI—Cheek-Rub
Hōzuri could be literally translated as "cheeksturbation" (it is a contraction of *hō*, "cheek," and *senzuri*, "masturbation"). In the nineties, with increasing fear of AIDS, clients often prefer to avoid being

fellated. In these cases the *seikan* girl services the organ with her hand and, for an added touch, rubs her cheek against its shaft.

In rougher institutions, such as Aoyama Biryō in Tokyo's Gotanda District, the client lies on his stomach with his legs apart, while the woman performs *anaru hōzuri* (anal cheek-rub).

KAME-SAN-GOROSHI SĀBISU—Killing-Mr.-Turtle Service

Kame (turtle) is a favorite earthy reference to the male organ. "Killing Mr. Turtle" is performed in three stages. First the *seikan* girl slips the usual lubricated *yubisakku* (finger sack) onto her left middle finger, and with small digging jabs penetrates her client from behind. As the penetration intensifies, she reaches with her right hand between his legs for his testicles in what is known as *bōruzuri purē* (literally "ball-sturbation play"). In the climactic stage of this service the woman grabs Mr. Turtle—the customer's penis—and incites orgasm by forcefully wringing and squeezing it with throttling hand motions.

KANOKE PURĒ—Coffin Play

Coffin play is among the most intense and exclusive programs available at the *seikan* parlors. The client lies on the mat and is approached by three women. Two of them lie down with him, one on each side, while the third covers him from the top like the lid of a coffin. Enclosed in this expensive casket, the client is penetrated, manipulated, and licked. In some parlors this same service is offered as *osōshiki* (funeral).

When even more *seikan* girls are called in to work on a customer, the program is known as *manji sābisu* (whirling service). The more yen the client puts on the table, the more women whirl.

MAUSU SUPESHARU—Mouth Special
While the *seikan* girl fingers her client from behind, she simultaneously mouth-services him from the front. In some parlors, however, the woman divides the session into two neat parts; she will finger for the first half and then work orally for the second.

As the fear of AIDS increased in the early nineties, many *seikan* parlors took to *surippu* (slip), a contraction of "skin lip" or condomed fellatio.

NAISHIN-KYŌ SUPESHARU—Endoscope Special
Customers interested taking a closer look at their *seikan* girl's vagina are handed an authentic gynecologist's endoscope, with which they can study the organ to their heart's content.

The less sophisticated parlors offer the simpler *mushimegane sābisu* (magnifying glass service). The client looks intently through the glass while he is deftly brought to orgasm.

NIKAI-SEN—Two-Time Attack
The concept behind the two-time attack is that the customer can ask for a repeat performance without extra charge. In this intense 45-minute session the *seikan* girl immediately slips on her finger sack, penetrates the client, and sees to it that he climaxes within 20 minutes. She then quickly leaves the room for a five-minute tea break and, popping back in, asks if he wants another round. Most men thank the *seikan* girl and leave, giving her 20 minutes in which she can take on another client.

The more elegant parlors have extended the two-timing concept, and offer *suwappu sābisu* (swap service). The woman crams a full massage session into 20 minutes, leaves her exhausted client lying on the mat and, swapping with her colleague in the neighboring room, repeats her chore. In some parlors, such as the Pink Palace in Osaka, this is served up as *pātona chenji* (partner change).

NYŪYOKU PURĒ—Bathing Play

Many of the better *seikan* parlors have showering facilities in which the customer can wash before, and, depending on the intensity of the session, after the massage has ended. Some parlors effectively use the initial ten-minute shower period for a playful *sōgo arai* (mutual wash), in which client and *seikan* girl scrub each other's organs.

Some parlors also have tubs which they use to offer the more sophisticated *nyūyoku purē* (bathing play). The *seikan* girls might split the massage into two parts and mimic the rival soap ladies' washing techniques. The customer is stimulated in the tub and then climaxed with deeply penetrating manual massage on a mat. In a popular variation, also known as *yubune purē* (tub play) and *yokusō purē* (bath play), the customer remains in the water while the woman intensively penetrates, manipulates, and fellates.

NYŪHAFU SEMMON—New-Half Specialty

Both the *herusu* and the *seikan* industries have upgraded their menus by offering the more eccentric customer special masseuses. A fresh phenomenon of the nineties are the new-half massages. New-half refers to either sex-change health and *seikan* girls, or actual "she-males" who have not had the operation yet. A number of parlors also offer *debu senmon* (fatso specials) with particularly large *seikan* girls, and *rōjo senmon* (old lady specials) featuring grandmotherly prostate masseuses.

OGAMIKATA—Hands-Clasped-in-Prayer
When one prays to a Buddhist or a Shinto deity it is customary to place one's palms together and to quickly rub them up and down with small repetitive movements. As a *seikan* service, this gesture of devoted prayer takes on a sacrilegious twist. The *seikan* girl kneels by her client, clasps her palms softly over his organ, and with brisk pious rubs brings him to orgasm.

SAN-TEN SETTO—Triple Set
Triple set usually refers to a program where the *seikan* girl focuses on her customer's anus, testicles, and sex organ. Some *seikan* parlors offer *san-ten setto* where the woman removes her undergarments, and while she massages anus and organ the client is free to reach for her vagina.

In other establishments, however, these same types of triple-service are also facetiously given culinary names such as *sanshoku supesharu* (three-color special) which can refer to any dish with three ingredients.

SŌGO HŌSHI—Mutual Service
This service is for customers who enjoy giving what they get. The customer is issued a protective *yubisakku* (finger sack) and lying closely to the *seikan* girl penetrates her with it while she penetrates him. In some *seikan* parlors this service is known as *sōgo A-zeme*

(mutual A-attack). If vibrators are introduced, the program is known as *sōgo A-zeme baibu* (mutual A-attack vibe).

Many *seikan* parlors now also offer their more advanced clientele *gyaku seikan* (inverted erogenous massage). The *seikan* girl lies completely still while the customer begins with anal and ends with vaginal massage.

YOBAI GOKKO—Night-Crawl Game
In olden times, during rice festivals and special holiday occasions, young men would go on *yobai* (night-crawling) expeditions. With the village in deep slumber, they quietly crawled to houses with young single women and molested them while they slept.

The *seikan* parlors and even some of the *herusu* and soaplands have resuscitated this ancient rite and successfully brought it up to date. The client tiptoes through the parlor's hallway and carefully opens the door of the private room he has been directed to. The *seikan* girl, clad in imported frilly lingerie, lies on her massage mat. Her eyes are closed and she is snoring loudly. Quietly kneeling beside her, the client begins touching and fondling her while she sleeps on, for a good 15 minutes. The *seikan* girl then "wakes up" in a state of extreme arousal, swiftly slips on her finger sack, and begins penetrating the client's anus.

YUBI SŌNAME —Full Toe-Lick
The *seikan* parlors appropriated the *sōname* (full lick service) from the rival soapland and *herusu* menus, and developed it to suit their clients needs. The customer is given an initial shower with a careful *chin arai* (penile wash), followed by a careful *yubi arai* (toe

wash). He then lies back on the futon, his legs pulled up, while the *seikan* girl slips on her finger sack. While she penetrates him to stimulate his prostate gland, she licks his toes and works her way up past his knees to reach his organ.

ZENSHIN MITCHAKU—Full-Body Adhesion

The topless or naked *seikan* girl lies on her customer, rubbing him with her body while her fingers work over his anus, testicles, and organ.

5 • JAPANESE S&M

What distinguishes a Japanese S&M club from its Western counterparts is that the *ojōsama*, the "princesses," who work there with whips, chains, candle wax, and enema syringes, are polite, gentle, and civil to their customers. Topnotch Tokyo clubs like Sodom, Labyrinth, or Paradise feel that the masochist who pays $200, $300, and even $400 and up should be treated with deference, and only abused during the allotted time of bondage. The dominatrix is charming on the phone when she arranges an appointment. When her victim arrives she bows and smiles, chats pleasantly as he undresses, and, once he is naked, even ushers him with small head-bows into the shower. It is only after he has toweled himself down, slipped on his condom, and is ready to be bound and gagged that the *ojōsama* assumes her domineering role. The standard sign for the bondage session to begin is, "I am the Queen today, greet me properly."

The decor of a Japanese S&M club usually follows Western patterns, with heavy chains, handcuffs, and tortuous ropes hanging from ceilings and walls. Whips, the extremely popular cat-o'nine-tails, and other instruments that have been neatly disinfected and arranged hang on racks. The Japanese S&M establishment is divided into separate private rooms so that customer and dominatrix can work one on one.

Privacy, most clubs feel, is important, since customers are usually naked, aroused, and brought to orgasm towards the end of the session. Depending on the type of service desired one might choose anything from the *kangofu rūmu*, the nurse's room for enemas and other clinical games, to the *keimusho no gōmon shitsu*, the prison torture-chamber.

As the customer is being tied up, the careful princess first of all inquires whether he prefers to be tied by his wrists or around his biceps area. "Hanasode? Nagasode?" "Half-sleeve or full-sleeve?" She carefully wraps an expensive velvety fabric around the designated area so that the customer is comfortable, and to prevent the rope from rubbing against his skin in the event that he might want to writhe about. Some of the more sophisticated clubs also offer *tsuri* (suspension). The customer, tangled up in chains and ropes, is heaved towards the ceiling. In a popular special called *mushizeme no gōmon* (steam-attack torture), the dominatrix helps the client squeeze into a tight leather bodysuit, usually a couple of sizes too small, and then fits a skintight mask with only one little hole in it over his face. The client, gasping in agony, is then hoisted into the air and is left dangling, usually upside down. The dominatrix leaves the room. Most Tokyo S&M clubs, like Marionette in Higashi Gotanda, Peter Pan in Meguro, and Elegance in the Ikebukuro District, have an immense wardrobe of leather costumes that clients can rent, and some clients even bring their own special outfits from home. Club Justine even has a collection of modish dresses in case there are requests for *josō* (cross-dressing) or *josō rezu* (cross-dressing lesbian). In this the client gets to pretend that he is a girl being tormented and molested by a lesbian dominatrix. The strict rule, however, is that condoms have to be firmly twinged on to prevent accidents.

The *ojōsama* begins with *jobamuchi* (horseback whipping). She targets the customer's exposed buttocks, carefully pressing the whip down as it strikes the skin to prevent the lash from recoiling and leaving painful marks. While the client is tied up, the princess will graduate to *rōsoku zeme* (candle attacks). There are two types: *sofuto* (soft) which is the norm, and *hādo* (hard), which is doled out only to fanatics. For the common candle attack, the princess is careful to hold the candle horizontally, so that the relatively cool liquid wax drops onto the client's body, congealing painlessly into hard blobs. If the victim moans, "Ojōsama! Yakete, yakete!"—"Oh princess! Burn me, burn me!"—she will subject him to the "hard" version, in which the candle is held pointing down vertically so that the scalding wax drips sizzling through the flame onto his skin.

Another popular form of humiliation that the average Western dominatrix would recoil from in horror is the *anaru attaku* (anal attack). The princess first slips one condom over her index and middle fingers, and then for optimum hygiene glides on another. In all the better S&M parlors her double-condomed fingers are well-lubricated with petroleum jelly, while amateurish places (to the professionals' horror) go for lotion or even skin cream. She "attacks" her client, and when he is ready for deeper penetration she reaches for a dildo, pulls two protecting condoms over its shaft, and if it is an electric model flicks on the switch.

In Justine, one of the older and tougher Tokyo clubs near the Shibuya police precinct in the

Dōgenzaka area, the anal attack special culminates in *dōnyō* (forced peeing), and in some cases a forced bowel movement. Another Tokyo club, Aurora in Higashi Gotanda, takes the peeing specialties even further with games such as *ganmen shawa* (face showers) and *innyō* (pee imbibing). If the customer wishes to pee on a hostess, the fee for a 70-minute package comes to $280. If he prefers to be peed upon, the price is only $180. The dominatrix-in-charge at Tokyo's hard-core Queen in Nakano, in an interview with essayist Takasaki Makiko, confesses that when it comes to peeing on customers many of her younger dominatrixes panic and find themselves too jittery to let go. In these cases the *mama,* as she is known, has the lights turned down and asks the client to kindly avert his eyes from the girl squatting above him.

Many clubs, like Yumetono (Dream Lord) in the Ōtsuka District in Tokyo and Paradise in Ayase, are known for their *kanchō sābisu* (enema service). Paradise even offers a supervised defecation program as a follow-up. There is much rivalry among the clubs as to which offers the best enemas, but the dominatrixes at Queen are reputed to have refined their technique to the point that their enemas rival those administered at the nearby Holy Mother Hospital.

The enema is performed in three stages. The naked customer lies on a delivery table while a large syringe is filled with equal parts of warm water and glycerin. The contents are gently injected in mellow spurts until the syringe is empty. As the *ojōsama* removes the instrument she is very careful not to pull at the piston, as a vacuum at this delicate point could result in a violent reaction. In the elegant confines of the Queen club, the client is allowed to proceed to a private bathroom before the second enema, while at earthier establishments he might be ordered to retain the water and suffer, or worse, to relieve himself in full view of his tormentress. The customer then takes a shower and returns to the *ojōsama* who, syringe in hand, patiently waits by the delivery table. The second dosage is a warm and bubbly mixture of water and soap, and the client again sidles off to the bathroom and then to the shower. The third and last dosage is just warm water. At this point the more devil-may-care clients brave an excruciating trip home without the customary visit to the bathroom.

Many clubs, like Yumetono (Dream Lord), Justine, and Florence, have gone beyond whips, candles, and enemas, and cater to the *ōkii-akachan mania* (big-baby maniacs). These clubs have developed specialized services that are variously known as *yōji purē* (infant play), *bonyū purē* (mother's milk play), *akachan omutsu* (child diaper), or just *omutsu gēmu* (diaper games). With diapers and bibs tailored to fit even the heftiest clients, maternal dominatrixes spank, powder, breast-feed, and burp their charges for an average fee of $250 an hour. The idea behind most of the diaper games is that the dominatrix is trying, unsuccessfully, to toilet-train her big baby. She breast feeds him, he does his bowel movement, and she, furious that he did not say *benki* (potty) changes and then spanks him severely for being a naughty boy. A surprising twist in most of these games is that towards the end of the allotted hour the "wet nurse" quickly turns into a child-molester, massaging the freshly-diapered client to orgasm.

Being a masochist on the Japanese scene is much cheaper than being a sadist. In an average club, like

Reijō in Osaka, masochist customers pay $120, while the sadist who is interested in tying up and molesting girls, pays $180. In the more expensive Tokyo establishments, such as Thanks in Ikebukuro, the rate for masochists is $170 and for sadists $270. Caprice in Gotanda in Tokyo, which has a proud policy of firing all its girls on their twenty-fifth birthdays, charges sadists $280 and up. In the most serious and specialized bondage clubs like Miyabi, sadists who are interested in taking brutality a little further must first register at the reception at $280 and then pay as much as $680 for two hours of carte blanche. At that price, the club guarantees them an attractive S&M video actress between jobs.

The early nineties saw a massive surge in the interest in bondage. The superstar actress Yamasaki Senri came out with a best-selling photo album, in which she exposes herself to millions of adoring fans in outlandish bondage outfits, topless, and from angles that blatantly challenge the strict no-pubic-hair laws. (This brought her a warning from the Tokyo police commission.) She opened her own bondage boutique—*Madonna*—where the items were snatched off the shelves in a buying frenzy. Soon leather clothing, from underwear to evening gowns, was selling out in boutiques all over Japan. Then millions of TV watchers squealed in scandalized delight when Fuyuhiko, the leading man in the popular 1992 TV drama *Zutto anata ga suki datta* ("I Truly Loved You") gave his horrified wife bondage corsets as a present.

More and more S&M clubs, most of them bogus, opened to accommodate the rush of eager initiates. The *Fuyuhiko genshō* (Fuyuhiko phenomenon), as the media was now calling the unexpected S&M craze, was fired up by the arrival in December, 1992 of the Japanese version of Madonna's book *SEX*, which to everyone's surprise had largely escaped censorship.

S&M was turning into a gold mine, and sex-trade establishments from *herusu* to soaplands scrambled in a race to be the first to add bondage to their programs. Flexible parlors like Bijo no Yakata (The House of Beautiful Women) and Aoi Gensō (Blue Fantasy) had successfully expanded from "health massage" to "pressure-point massage" and were now raking in the yen by launching themselves as semi-S&M specialists. Joshiryō (Women's Dormitory) offered its clients *uomingu-appu purē* (warming-up play), with frontal and rear pressure-point manipulation. Once the client is fully excited, the masseuse becomes, on request, either a *Sadisu-chan* (little Miss Sadist) or a *dorei* (slave). Purple, one of the more ritzy soaplands in Yoshiwara, Tokyo's old red-light district, went all-out and became Japan's first $500-a-wash sado-masochistic bathhouse.

As more and more men were interested in trying S&M, agencies like Chateau and Rei hired dominatrixes and female slaves for house-calls, while Slave Market Planning and Dark Crystal dispatched packs of "S-boys," "M-boys," and "normal boys." The mission of these agencies was to cater to clients of every persuasion. S&M boys and girls traveled for miles by train, bus, boat or even plane in order to reach long-distance callers from remote mountain villages.

The expensive Chateau agency, with its central location in the Shibuya District in Tokyo, does much of its work in downtown hotels, as many of its clients are well-to-do businessmen with wives waiting at home. All of the girls that Chateau sends out are certified to be both sadistic and masochistic. The businessman calls, the demure switchboard operator suggests the double special of the day, names a top hotel, and adds, "Please be there in 20 minutes." The "double" turns out to be two refined and superbly dressed women. Following the routine, the girls slip out of their evening gowns and bondage leather-panties, and lure the naked businessman into the bathroom. All three squeeze into the narrow hotel shower, vigorously soap, scrub, rinse and towel each other down, and then, refreshed, topple into the twin bed. The girls reach for their purses to get out their compact leather whips, and start flogging each other gently. At this point, the customer has the option of either relaxing on his own, helping the girls whip each other, or offering up himself to be whipped. The girls help him climax before they leave on another mission.

For men who prefer a somewhat raunchier challenge the delivery agency of choice is the Bad Boy

Kikaku (Bad Boy Project). The bad boy in this case is not the customer, but the boy dispatched by the agency, which prides itself on its high standing among urban Japan's most hard-core S&M networks. The boy ties up his client and whips him. He is an expert at *supankingu* (spanking) fellatio, sodomy, and, if the client requests the house special, *shiōzumi shitagi kōsu* (used-underpants course), during which he is free to chew at the boy's jockstrap while he is being serviced.

REAL S&M

The true bondage cognoscenti have stayed away from what by international S&M standards would be denounced as blatant charlatanism. Fanatics who had been practicing sadomasochism long before the nationwide craze began in the late eighties continued attending their members-only clubs. One of the most exclusive of these places, the Discipline Gym in Yotsuya in Tokyo, has strictly limited its membership to 200 initiates. Newcomers are subjected to grueling interviews and close screenings. The Discipline Gym novice must be a person with strong creative tendencies (artists are given preference), and must be a true *hentai* (pervert), preferably a fetishist. Only the loftiest perversions, however, are acceptable, for members caught drinking and whipping or displaying signs of sexual arousal find themselves instantly expelled.

Another strict members-only club that prides itself on catering to diehard sadists and masochists is Sodomu no Ichi (The Site of Sodom). It was founded in Osaka in the late seventies by Ms. Hanamai, a retired S&M porn star. By the mid-eighties business was so good that she opened a branch in Tokyo, boosting her membership into the thousands. The Site of Sodom works more like an agency than a club. It organizes get-togethers, parties, galas and even S&M field trips to scenic hot-spring resorts. Unlike Tokyo's Discipline Gym, it is relaxed about its members' moral standards, and the membership requirements are simple enough. One has to be able to afford the initiation fee ($180 for women, $280 for men), one has to be over 20, and one has to be a practicing heterosexual—at the first sign of homosexuality initiates are defrocked. The Site of Sodom members meet on an average of twice a month in designated apartments in Tokyo and Osaka, in small groups of not more than ten men and ten women. Members also meet in hotels, slinking from one room to another in intricate bondage games with multiple partners.

Another hard-core club that started in Osaka in the eighties and expanded successfully to Tokyo is the Kuro no Kai (Hard Bottom Association). In this club, anything goes as long as it is strictly *man-tsu-man* (man-to-man). No women are permitted on the premises, and the only heterosexual males allowed are the young college-jock models. They are hired on a monthly basis as a special *non-ke* (non-gay) delicacy for the members, who get to engage them in gropey wrestling matches. Those interested in molesting the young heterosexual in private can do so at an extra charge of $200.

Most members would describe themselves as *shirizuki mania* (bottom-fanatic maniacs), men with a bottom fixation, and true to its name, the club goes to extremes to provide hard bottoms for its members. At its meetings one can opt for *supankingu* (spanking), *shiri no aibu* (bottom caressing), even *anusu name* (anal licks). *Taiiku gakusei* (sports students) are brought in for special *shiriuchi shō* (bottom-whipping shows), after which members can grope them to their hearts' content.

Sadists, masochists, and fetishists who wish to combine homosexual bondage and travel, can check in at a number of new S&M hotels. In a country flooded with Western tourists, these sanctuaries have the added attraction that they lock their doors to all foreigners and individuals of mixed Japanese race. One of the first major S&M Hotels in Nagoya was the Dombara Kaikan. It stood on the dreary banks of the Hori River near the Naya Bridge, and has recently moved across the water and three blocks south, to reopen with a bang as the even bigger Corona.

The original hotel had been a boisterous 60-room institution, nine stories high, with the gay bar Adon no Bara (Adonis' Rose) in the basement (the contraction of which, Dombara, was chosen as the hotel's name). Weary travelers and venturesome locals mingled in the men-only restaurant, the sex-baths, and in the private and public S&M play rooms. There was even a whole floor (the eighth) cordoned off for traveling transvestites. The formula was so successful, that the new 64-room Corona Hotel was set up along the same lines, roping in even more clients with its modern pools, extended parking, and frisky threesome massages.

The more modest S&M inns, such as Tabarishi in downtown Hiroshima, offer similar floor-by-floor service. Here too thoroughbred Japanese sadists and masochists are guaranteed a racially pure environment and can unwind in the S&M saunas on the second floor, or in the bondage rooms on the third. In Tabarishi, the friskier client can check himself into the no-questions-asked *inran rūmu* (slut rooms) on the fourth floor.

Japanese homosexual and heterosexual bondage have developed largely along the same lines. Clubs like the Discipline Gym and The Site of Sodom also cater to women with sadistic or masochistic tastes, but in most places S&M is male-oriented, with women merely fulfilling the customers' needs by taking on the roles of dominatrix or slave. Very few clubs accept lesbian clients. One aspect, however, in which the male homosexual S&M scene sets itself apart, is that its motifs and bondage ideals are on the whole more Japanese in inspiration. A Western masochistic ideal might be a big man in leather wielding whips and chains; the popular Japanese equivalent would be the *irezumi otoko* (tattoo man), whose full-body tattoos identify him as a tough and dangerous Yakuza gang member. Many Japanese masochists will pay good money to be tortured by a real Yakuza man, and specialized clubs hire tattooed men for their clients. Triple-X video corporations like B-Product and Anuxxs churn out blockbuster S&M titles such as *Irezumi-ana jigoku—kezori* ("Shaving—The Tattoo-hole Hell").

In the Japanese-style S&M bars, clients sit on tatami mats, drink steaming rice wine, and engage in tough, risqué banter. They are naked except for a fiercely traditional *fundoshi*, a loosely-tied loincloth. Bars like Tokyo's Ikioi and Sada in Nagoya City, have private rooms in the back, so that the clients can whip each other after a few drinks. To capture moments from these memorable occasions, management, for a fee, offers its customers *pora-sābisu* (polaroid service).

Traditional Japanese S&M clubs can usually be spotted by their traditional names. While a Western-style club might bill itself with a fetching Marquis de Sade-inspired name like Justine, or Labyrinth, the club that seeks sadistic inspiration in Japan's distant past, might opt for names like Miyabi or Rashōmon. The dominas and the slaves wear elegant kimonos and white make-up on their faces and necks. The Rashōmon parlor has developed its traditional motifs in many directions. Its strong point is catering to traditional transvestites who wish to be tormented while dressed in full formal regalia, from kimono and exquisite wig to delicate Edo Period hairpins. Another popular Rashōmon delicacy is its intricate *jukujo senka* (mature-woman special). The elderly hostess that is called in to service the client assumes, on request, such roles as the avenging mother, or the tortured grandmother. The house specialty, however, is served up in the club's main private room, labeled *Onna Seppuku no Satsuei Koshitsu* (Private Female Harakiri Screening Room). Here customers can watch a beautiful but desperate woman in medieval garb elegantly take her own life.

THE S&M MENU

A-NAME—A-lick

A-name is short for *anusu name* (anal lick). It is a highly prized and hard-to-find humiliation offered by hard-core bondage clubs such as the heterosexual Aurora and Marionette in Tokyo's Gotanda District, and the homosexual Kuro no Kai (Hard Bottom Association) in Osaka. In some of the earthier clubs it is also offered under the guise of *uraname sābisu* (ass-lick service).

Usually it is the masochist who pays to be ordered to lick, but in certain situations, as in Aurora's deluxe "true masochist girl program" ($780) the customer, for two hours, is king.

ANARU ZEME—Anal Attack

Depending on the establishment, anal attacks come in every shape and size. Fingers, toes, boot-heels, strings of cultured pearls—anything might be used. The motto is: surprise your masochist and he will come back for more. In many of the heterosexual establishments a typical *sofuto* (soft) attack is the *anaru muchi* (anal whip). After the princess has spent the first portion of the allotted time lashing her client, she will stretch a condom over the rod-end of her whip and gently begin spiking away. An even more common approach is the *anaru baibu zeme* (anal vibe attack), in which a vibrator is used.

The more venturesome masochists, however, turn to fetish-friendly clubs like Reiga in Tokyo for hard-driving services such as *pinhiiru sōnyū* (stiletto heel penetration). The client lies face down while the princess, leaning back on her elbows by his feet, tromps her spiky heel into him. In other instances, a high-heeled princess might subject her slave to an excruciating *haihiiru-bumi* (high heel walk), in which she will stomp over him as he lies, tied up and defenseless, on his back.

For the ultimate attack the S&M princess, depending on how strict she is, orders her client to auto-insert a medium, large, or extra large *dendō puragu* (electric plug). After she has been obeyed, she presses the button to start it expanding, quaking, and vibrating at different speeds.

ASHI NAME—Foot Licking

Many clubs offer services for what is known in S&M circles as either the *ashi-ma* (foot devil) or the *ashi mania* (foot maniac). *Ashi name*, also known in its anglicized version as *futu sakkingu* (foot sucking) or *futu purē* (foot play), usually entails the customer being allowed to lick an "S" girl's or an "S" boy's feet.

Clubs that cater to foot-specialists usually also offer *kutsu name* (shoe licking), and have large closets of women's shoes on hand. The customer selects his favorite shoe model, and the dominatrix slips into a pair. Club Reiga in Tokyo even has a choice of *gakusei gutsu*, shoes that very young schoolgirls wear with their uniforms.

Other places, like Tokyo's Justine, Yumetono, or Miyako also cater to clients who enjoy wearing women's shoes while tied up, whipped, or dangling from the ceiling.

ASHI-ZURI—Foot Masturbation

Ashi-zuri is to Japanese what "foot-sturbation" would be to English. It is an amalgam of *ashi* (foot) and *zuri* (rub, as in *senzuri* or "masturbation"). The S&M princess deftly wedges a customer's sexual organ between her feet, and brings him to orgasm with gentle rhythmic tugs. A popular foot-fetishist synonym for this practice is *ash-tabēshon*, a fusion of *ashi* (foot) and *masutabēshon*, the Japanese pronunciation of "masturbation."

CHIKUBI ZEME—Nipple Assault

In the Japanese S&M world there are two distinct schools of nipple assault. In the softer of the two, the naked client lies face down and legs apart while a topless princess uses her nipple to stimulate and penetrate. In harsher parlors the target is the customer's nipple. Depending on a masochist's tolerance, his nipple may be exposed to anything from *rō* (dripping candle wax) to *chikubi no shimegane* (nipple clamps), with possible on-site nipple piercing.

S&M parlors also cater to clients who enjoy manhandling girls' breasts. In a program that the bondage scene refers to as *nyūtō ijime* (woman's nipple torment), the sadist can whip, bite, and squeeze his topless S&M hostesses' breasts.

CHŌKYŌ—Training

Chōkyō (training) in S&M parlors and clubs includes all the sadistic and the masochistic services. The masochist is the *uma* (horse), the *inu* (dog), the *osu inu* (male dog), the *genan* (manservant) or even the *dorei* (slave), and he pays top yen for the dominatrix or master to subject him to grueling *chōkyō*. This can involve his being tied up and whipped, urinated or defecated upon, or simply wearing a tight *inu no kubiwa* (dog collar). In the more recondite members-only clubs, *chōkyō* can also involve subtle humiliation, like having to shop for and try on frilly panties in large department stores.

The modern Japanese sadist can also turn to S&M clubs to provide him with the perfect *Shinobu-chan* (little Miss Tolerance), *gejo* (maid) or *omocha* (toy). The more money he pays, the stricter the training he can inflict.

Many of the more serious S&M clubs, like Tokyo's heterosexual Elegance, or Osaka's homosexual SDM Daimon, offer workshops and special introductory courses for eager but inexperienced sadists and masochists. This is known as *shinjin chōkyō* (newcomer training). Step by step the novice is trained by a patient specialist who demonstrates the ABC's of whip and chain.

DŌJI ZEME—Simultaneous Attack

In most sex clubs, *dōji* service implies that the customer is allowed to reciprocate the type of manipulation or massage that he is receiving. In S&M clubs, however, *dōji zeme* (simultaneous attack) refers to *dōji kanchō* (simultaneous enema). The customer and the dominatrix approach each other, each with an enema syringe in hand.

ERUBO ATAKKU—Elbow Attack

Erubo attaku, the Japanese pronunciation of the English "elbow attack," is a masochistic delicacy in which a bondage princess pounds, and sometimes even penetrates, the client's anus with her elbow. The elbow attack has been a long-standing favorite in some of the rougher soapland bathhouses as well, where it is sometimes served up under its original Japanese name *hiji zeme* (elbow assault).

The masochist seeking stronger stimulation might opt for the *genkotsu zeme* (fist assault), in which the anus is assaulted with a tightly clenched fist. The ultimate bondage penetration is the *hiza zeme* (knee assault). The princess grinds and prods while massaging her client's organ at the same time. In some of the more fashion-conscious S&M parlors this special is available under the hybrid Anglo-Japanese name *nii zeme* (joining the English word "knee" to *zeme*, "assault").

GANMEN KIJO ZEME—Facial Horseback Attack
The sadistic princess ties up her naked client's arms and legs, and rolls him onto his back. Unbuttoning her leather leotard she seats herself heavily on his face and begins riding it, prodding his penis with her whip as she rocks back and forth. In opulent parlors like Tokyo's Labyrinth this service is priced at $220, plus the $90 registration fee.

GYAKU FUNSHA—Inverted Jet
The S&M princess seizes the masochist's organ, arouses it, and gently inserts a straw. She mixes a beaker of warm water with glycerin, and carefully pours the liquid into the straw, while the customer writhes in pleasure.

HARI IJIME—Needle Taunting
Some S&M parlors offer specialized princesses and bondage masters who taunt their masochistic customers with disinfected needles. (The Queen club in the Nakano District in Tokyo guarantees that all its attacks are executed with fresh, unused needles). The masochist is first bound and then pricked and jabbed on his arms and thighs, a practice that many parlors also call *hari zeme* (needle attack). Serious customers also have their ears, noses, eyebrows, lips, and nipples pierced. The toughest masochist goes even further; he requests that the princess perform the needle attack on his foreskin and, in some extreme cases, the shaft of his organ.

In a much more dangerous variation—the *chūshaki zeme* (syringe attack)—the princess plays doctor. Carefully wielding a fresh needle, she painfully injects small squirts of liquid into her customer's erogenous zones.

KOGANE MIZU—Golden Water

In Western bondage circles the *kogane mizu sābisu* (golden water service) is known as golden showers. The dominatrix squats over her customer and lets a flush of golden water drench his face. In some hardcore clubs the golden water is also known as *ōgonsui* (gold water).

With the release of video hits such as the Anuxxs Corporation's *Ōgonsui jigoku* (Gold Water Hell), this term has recently gained ground in some of the rougher homosexual bondage circles. The video features tough and tattooed gangsters on a vicious rampage. They tie each other up and engage in merciless beating and raping, which is then followed by jet upon jet of gold water.

In more polished sadomasochistic circles like Tokyo's Club Aurora, these water-games are known as *ganmen shawa* (face showers). Other parlors in Tokyo, such as Miyajima, prefer the stricter technical term *hōsui* (water-spouting).

The most drastic masochists kneel in abject veneration before their expensive S&M princess and beg her for *osei-sui* (sacred water). When the steaming stream of liquid hits their faces, some careful clients pinch their lips tightly shut. Others, however, require their dominatrix to force them at whip-point to undergo *nyō-ugai* (urine gargle), and finally even *innyō* (imbibing of urine).

KUSUGURI SĀBISU—Tickling Service

One of the most excruciating sadistic S&M programs entails a tickling that leaves no part of the masochist untouched. The princess starts with his heel and works her way up, usually with a featherduster. A particularly grueling version of this torture is *oshiri no kusuguri* (bottom tickle), often referred to more graphically as *anusu no kusuguri* (anal tickle).

MANGESORI GĒMU—Shaving Game

The masochist watches the S&M princess shave her pubic area, and in some expensive cases is even allowed to shave it for her. *Mange* is an earthy reference to a woman's pubic hair, originating from *man* (cunt) and *ge* (hair). In the more elegant bondage clubs, this same service is available either as *kezori* (hair-shave) or under the proper S&M name *teimō* (hair-shearing). Most clubs, like Estele in Gotanda, have trained girls who work on clients in what is known as *zenshin teimō* (full-body hair-shearing).

In the hard-core homosexual bondage parlors, shaving is referred to as *chingesori* (penile-hair shaving, *chinge* being a fusion of *chinpo* (penis) and *ge* (hair). Private clubs organize special public pubic shaving events known as *teimō enkai* (hair-shearing galas). In front of cheering crowds, members file one by one onto a podium or a small makeshift stage, where a specialist with a razor awaits them.

ŌMATA-BIRAKI—Thigh-Wrench

Thigh-wrenching is one of the more dangerous of the popular S&M programs. In its most expensive version, the paying sadist first carefully ties up his S&M club hostess. Depending on the club, he might then whisk off the defenseless hostess's panties, and, grabbing her by the ankles, discipline her by wrenching her legs as far apart as they go.

Other thigh-wrenching options call for the S&M princess to force open her customer's thighs while she might jab at him with dildos and whip-rods.

SUPANKINGU SĀBISU—Spanking Service

The spanking service is the crux of every modern Japanese S&M parlor. The customer is tied up, his pants are yanked down, and the dominatrix starts spanking him with her bare palm, a special plastic mini-paddle, or a wooden bat. In "spanking M-play" the customer gets to be the masochist, while in the more expensive "spanking S-play", he is the aggressor. In many clubs throughout Japan professional spanking is also known as *ketsu-tataki* (ass-beating), *ketsu-uchi* (ass-hitting), and *ketsu-naguri* (ass-walloping). Once the customer is safely tied up, the punishing S&M princess will bark, "Ketsu-tataki jū kai!"—"Ten ass-lashes for you!"—and the action begins.

When the customer is the sadist, the bondage girl will usually play the role of an innocent prepubescent girl, whose de-pantied bottom is being chastised by a strict paternal disciplinarian. For this type of games softer terms, like *oshiri penpen*, (bottom smackety-smack) and *oshiri ponpon* (bottom slapety-slap) are favored.

SHIBARI—Tying Up

The most important ingredients for a successful S&M stint are the ropes, chains, and gags (known as *kuchidome*, "mouth stoppers" and *sarugutsuwa*, "monkey muzzles"). The Western dominatrix inspecting a fashionable Japanese parlor would be surprised at the delicate rope-work that her Japanese peers engage in. What would surprise her even more is that the sadistic ropes are often color-coordinated in pleasant pinks and blues, and that the princess takes great pains to tie them in deft criss-cross patterns.

In some of the "soft" parlors specializing in *mūdii-S* (moody sadism), the colorful ropes smack suspiciously of silk hair ribbons. They are often tied so lightly that one uncautious movement on the masochist's part is enough to loosen them.

In more serious S&M circles, the ropes and chains are sturdier. The princess who specializes in *kōsoku M-sābisu* (restricted masochist service) ties her knots according to the endurance capacity of her client. She will even ask, "Kizuato o nokoshimashō ka?"— "Would you be interested in lesions?" In all the better parlors the *mama*, or domina-in-chief, supervises her flock of young princesses until their tying techniques are up to scratch.

In Nagoya City, homosexual sadists interested in studying the art of rope-tying can join technical workshops at club Sabu. Every third Sunday, from 3 p.m. to 6 p.m., a certified *nawashi* (rope master) offers free lecture demonstrations and one-on-one instruction.

SHŪCHI PURĒ—Bashful Play
This play is the part of the S&M session where the sadistic princess torments the bashful masochist with embarrassing commands. She will, for instance, tell him to lick her shoes, play with himself while she watches, and, depending on the parlor, even demand that he let her pee on him.

6 • PINK SALONS

Among all the sex-trade parlors the pink salons offer the cheapest, most casual, and most rapid orgasms in all of Japan. The salons are musty and loud, with row upon row of *bokkusu seki* (box seats), small private compartments designed like plush restaurant booths. Here customers are groped, jabbed, rubbed, and licked by pink hostesses at $25, $45 and up—the sessions vary from salon to salon—lasting anywhere from 15 to 40 minutes. There is no sex (except in the illegal *honban saron*, "performance salons"), but the hostesses compete with the rival soaplands, *herusu*, and *seikan* women. They even snatched from them staple services like *paizuri* (breast-urbation) and *sukochi-fera* (scotch fellatio). In the cramped box seats, however, even the wildest *herusu*, *seikan*, or S&M tricks take on a special *pinku-chikku* (pink-esque) flavor, since everything from simple massage to complex anal-vibrator play has to be carried out in a sitting, or at best leaning position.

The box seats all face out onto the dark club corridor, where hostesses scurry between booths through lines of men entering and leaving the salon. This layout insures that customers will not have to sit opposite other customers while they are in session. The compartments are flimsily separated from each other either by wooden half-partitions or by clumps of artificial trees and shrubbery. The lights are turned so low that hostesses and clients can barely see each other, but hanging mirror-balls send flashes of light through the booths, and men waiting for their hostesses can check on neighboring compartments by standing on tiptoe or carefully peeking through the plastic undergrowth.

The pink salons are registered at their local police stations as *ichi-ryōin kankei eigyō* (businesses of food and drink), so in deference to the law each booth has a table with a dusty liquor bottle and two empty glasses on it, one for the hostess and one for the client. No one, however, drinks.

The anonymity, the open space, and especially the darkness of these salons attract specific kinds of hostesses. Many younger women, such as students with credit card debts or desperate housewives, feel more comfortable working in an open space where a screech will bring the waiters running. Given the rapid turnover of customers, these hostesses can earn thousands of dollars a month, marginally less than their peers in the more expensive parlors, without having to expose their bodies to the bright bulbs of the *herusu*, *seikan*, and soaplands. As a result, women who are heavy, unattractive, old, or simply too shy to work elsewhere are not discriminated against.

Many urban pink salons provide *joshiryō* (women's dormitories) to encourage an influx of small-town women who are eager to come to the big cities. Every spring, millions of yen are invested in "we have a dormitory" ads, and in early summer, before the provincial colleges have even closed for vacation, hordes of liberated students ready for *arubaishun* (*arubaito-baishun* or "part-time prostitution") descend on big-city salons. Outside the salons lines of men impatiently await the seasonal *rorikon supesharu* (Lolita-complex special).

The pink salons encourage *shimei* (nomination), where for the usual $10 to $15 fee the customer requests a specific woman. The more requests, the higher the hostess' ratings, and the more yen she earns. Computerized pink salons keep ratio charts on their hard drives. Depending on both the number of men and nominations, star hostesses are awarded an "A," while slacker women are given a "B," "C," or "D." Women who are requested less than five times in one week are given an "E" along with a warning. If the pink computer prints out an "F," the hapless hostess must resign.

The philosophy behind these harsh policies is that the pink hostess, desperate to keep her job, will undoubtedly try to hook her customers into coming back; even if it means promising *umanori* (horse riding), in which, riding the fully-dressed customer's lap, she permits the illegal "connection of the sex-organs."

Outside the pink salon are posters with bold messages like "69" and "ANAL." Unlike the more expensive *herusu* and soaplands, the pink salon's entrance is lined with polaroid shots of the women, all wearing heavy dark glasses. Customers can ask the *pōtā* (porter) who stands beckoning in the street specific questions like prices, bust size, and who is good at what.

As the client enters he is met by a whiff of perfume, followed by a second whiff of disinfectant mixed with a powerfully stale stench. Most salons today offer a *pakku ryōkin* (package fee). The customer pays an all-inclusive sum at the desk, is issued a number, and is directed by loudspeaker to a booth. The fee covers manual stimulation and the climactic fellatio, and also includes minor specials like *bōru name* (ball-lick or testicle licking), *oppai kusuguri* (breast tickling), and the popular *buisain* (V-sign). In this last, the customer makes the victory sign with his index and middle fingers and penetrates his hostess by slipping his hand under the elastic of her panties.

When the session is over and the hostess has wiped the client with the warm wet *oshibori* towels, he enters a phase known in the trade as *sutanbai* (standby), which means he must sit and wait for a loudspeaker announcement. Within minutes, a voice in full stereo calls out his number and bellows *panchi taimu!* (punch time), the pink jargon for "thank you, time's up." In some feisty salons the disk jockey will add a polite *omedetō gozaimasu* (congratulations), followed by *hosutessu, bakku!* (hostess, back to base). A waiter flits into the booth and using salad-tongs piles the soiled towels onto a tray, while the floor manager inspects the booth with a flashlight.

Clients wishing to stay for more must pay a *nominaoshi-ryo* (drink-correction fee).

At the lower end of the pink salon scale are the seedier establishments that do not have the straight-forward package fee that today's client has come to expect. These salons are known on the street as the *bottakuri saron* (rip-off salons). Their supporters argue that they are crusading against the *beruto konbeya gata* (conveyor-belt mentality) of their sister-salons, where lines of clients are herded into booths for their pre-packaged 25 minute sessions. An a la carte salon such as Trendy in Tokyo will charge the basic $40 fee, allow the client to relax with his hostess for as long as he wishes, and then confront him with an additional itemized bill as he makes his way to the door. These places also offer an option known as "fruits date." The customer pays a large fee at the reception desk and can take a favorite pink hostess out for dinner or to the theater.

The pink salons originated in Osaka. Like their rivals the soaplands, they sprang out of the turmoil of the post-World War II era. Their immediate ancestors were the *ozashiki kissa* (parlor cafes) and the *tatami kissa* (tatami-mat cafes), in which customers would arrive in groups to be entertained by the *sao-hime* (rod-princesses). They would have a drink or two, engage in risqué badinage known as *uai* ("Y" for *yarashii*, "indecent talk") and *shimoneta* (arousing-what's-down-there), and the party would end with manual stimulation. In the following decades these cafes developed into pink pubs, pink theaters, pink lounges, pink cabarets, and pink salons. Common to all these establishments was that paying customers were ensured their orgasm.

By the seventies, the pink salon industry was flourishing in spite of constant police raids and a marked decline in the quality of service. The hostesses were growing more leathery, the reeky booths smaller and darker, but come opening time at 5:30 in the afternoon enthusiastic men would form long orderly lines that wound around the block. Salons were enticing their clients with bargain-priced *honban* ("on the air," or sex) and the police would invade.

By the early eighties the pink salons had achieved the blackest image among all the sex-trade parlors. A new breed of salon-magnate—the *Yū-bōto* (U-boats)—emerged. As his establishment was being raided by the police, he would be in the back room cramming yen notes into suitcases. Clutching his loot he would hastily "submerge" in the underworld, re-emerging within days to open a new salon elsewhere. To help the U-boats make smooth transitions, special agencies known as *pinku-kaitenya* (pink-shop-starting establishments) were set up. These brokered everything from placing strategic magazine ads and wining, dining, and massaging scandal-sheet writers, to arranging the bouquet of expert hostesses that would work the salon on opening night.

While the owners usually made their getaway during police raids, hostesses "horse riding" clients in dark booths often found they could not yank their panties up in time and run. Booked, cuffed, and dragged down to the precinct, they would be slapped with a small fine, a don't-ever-do-that-again warning, and sent back out onto the street. A hostess who is booked three times is known by her colleagues as *bentōmochi* (carrying a packed lunch). If she is caught one more time she will no longer need to carry a lunchbox; she'll be locked up and the state will provide it for her.

Since 1985, when the new Act to Control Businesses Which May Affect Public Morals was passed, the pink salon industry has worked on cleaning up its image. Its popularity ratings had plummeted as customers' tastes veered in the eighties towards the *shirōto gyaru* (amateur gals). The schoolgirl look was in, and even hostesses in their forties, emboldened by the dark, bravely slipped into gym skirts and high school uniforms, gasping a frightened "Iya!" (Oh no!) when clients touched their knee. Many of the older women proved themselves masters at both acting wide-eyed and confused, while still managing to successfully climax their customers within the ordained 20 minutes. In an interview with a pink salon owner, the writer and social critic Kakinuma Chisato was surprised to hear that his most popular hostess was 55.

The new and inexperienced hostess is known as the *momo* (thighs). For the first three days she is being broken in, she is only required to rub the customer's *momo*. In a 20-minute stint, the trainee stays for 15 minutes with the client in his booth, and he can touch

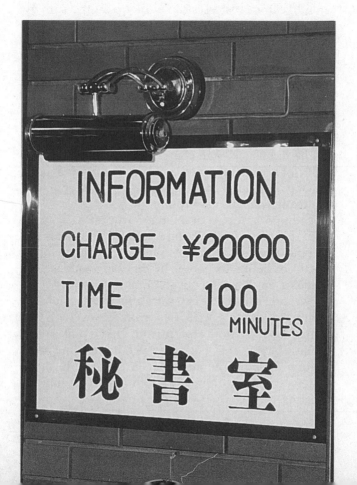

her breasts. When it is "flower time," the final climactic five minutes, the trainee leaves and an experienced woman finishes him off. The pink salon maxim is: *Mata mikka—kaki yōka*, "Three days, thighs—eight days, hand-job."

The pink hostesses are usually paid every two weeks. The average rate in the mid-nineties was $100 a day, with an additional $5 per session. If she is nominated by a customer, she will earn between $5 and $10 extra. Hostesses can work up quite a sum by bobbing in and out of cubicles. In a typical pink salon like Lime House in Osaka, the woman steps into the booth, chats bashfully with the client for about two minutes, and then, cleaning him with the wet and steamy *oshibori* towels that she happens to be carrying, embarks on immediate "lip service" (fellatio). Within five minutes the customer falls exhausted back onto the sofa, the schoolgirlish hostess whispers, "I'll be right back" and charges out to a neighboring booth for a quick intermediate stint. Ten minutes later she pops her head back in and asks, "Are you sure you really want another round?"

An important part of the modern pink salon program is *hanabira kaiten* (petal rotation). The petals are the pink hostesses, and they rotate in 20-minute intervals from booth to booth. In this way, salons like Shinjuku Eapōto Nigoten (Shinjuku Airport #2) in Tokyo and Fruits Lady in Osaka offer their customers 40-minute sessions with two women and two orgasms. An even more enterprising Tokyo pink salon, the Blue Sky in the Ōtsuka District, has a triple petal rotation system. The customer is exposed to three hostesses who continuously booth-hop at ten-minute intervals.

Like all the sex-trade parlors, the pink salons have had to keep up a flow of new hostesses and new ideas. As soapland bathhouses and *herusu* parlors are doing less well, many soap ladies and health girls do *dyūda* (changing from one sex-trade branch into another) to pink salons. The experienced newcomers introduced a fresh wave of services to the salons. Some parlors, like the Banana Club in Tokyo's Kabukichō District, even have special *seikan* girls with their finger sacks carrying out prostate massage in the booths. Regular clients pay $40, prostate clients $120. The Banana Club customer can even ask for "bicycle," and two pink hostesses appear in his cubicle. In Nagoya, the Yūmin and the notorious Lip Cream absorbed so many *herusu* services into their menus that they re-launched themselves as *saron do herusu* (salon de health). The health body-licks, health breast-urbation, health *soixante-neuf*, even all-nude service, were all superimposed onto the pink salon system and adapted to fit the cramped booths, with their plush sofas and tables.

With the economy unstable, the recession growing, and all the competing sex-parlors racking their brains for innovative twists, pink salons looked around for hot new gimmicks. Candy in Tokyo turned up its lights, made its booths more comfortable and Western, really served drinks, and required all hostesses to start their session with a friendly *diipu kissu* (tongue kiss). The Akatombo (Firefly) in Osaka looked to Japan's past for inspiration. It rolled out the tatami mats, installed red paper lanterns, and surprised clients in their booths with steaming *sake*. Another salon nearby, the Time Machine, made a killing by establishing its own outlandish pink setup. Its premises are divided into three levels, each with its own strict rules and a $65 entrance fee. On the first floor the hostess sits still while the customer can touch her breasts. On the second floor he can run his fingers down into her panties. On the ultimate floor, after he has plunked down almost $200, she finally brings in the wet *oshibori* towels, disinfects his organ, and then fellates him.

Some even zanier clubs, like Futago no Kyabetsu (Twin Cabbage) and Yūjin Rando (Play-People Land), pull in customers by installing karaoke systems into the booths. Microphone in hand, men can sing to their favorite tunes while pink hostesses work on them. In Osaka, 11 Chanel acquired a sizable wardrobe of costumes and sent its hostesses to the booths one week as executive secretaries, the next as junior high schoolers. Jan Jan in Kanagawa outside Tokyo decided to ignore the AIDS threat and specialize in uncondomed fellatio. For the customer's peace of mind, all hostesses are tested for HIV twice a month.

Throughout all the cataclysmic changes of the late eighties and early nineties in the pink industry, the roughest and toughest salons have hung onto their old illegal habits. The *honban saron* ("on the air" salons) still entice their steady roster of clients with delicacies of illicit intercourse such as "throwing the net," "lasso," and "seesaw."

THE PINK MENU

BAIORENSU SĀBISU—Violence Service
This service could be termed both a quickie and a cheapie. If the client is pressed for time (e.g., is on a

lunch break), the pink hostess will move in on his penis without beating about the bush and frenetically massage away. Another name for intense but quick sessions is *tokkan kōji* (rush repair job).

FURENCHI KISSU SĀBISU—French Kiss Service

In America "French kiss" has been a popular allusion to tongue kissing since the 1920s, while "French style" has been a favorite euphemism for oral sex. The Japanese pink salon world combined these ideas. *Furenchi kissu* (French kiss) has come to refer to oral sex. By extension, French kiss service refers to massage that involves either the pink hostess fellating the client, the client cunnilinging the pink hostess, or both. This service also frequently appears in salons throughout Japan in the guise of the *gyaku sankaku gēmu* (upside-down triangle game). The triangles in this game are the customer and the hostess, who in the dark booth maneuver themselves into an upside-down position on the sofa.

HABURASHI SĀBISU—Toothbrush Service

In rowdier salons *haburashi* refers to fellatio. The concept is that the customer's organ, like a brush, rubs against the hostess's teeth. In pink salons that offer toothbrush without the customer having to wear a condom, the same special is upgraded to *hamigaki* (toothpaste).

If a customer prefers to climax on his hostess's face, the pink terminology is *karifurawā* (cauliflower). The inspiration for this salon expression comes from the image of sperm on the woman's face coagulating into bubbly white blobs reminiscent of little cauliflower stalks.

Other notable fellatio variations are *bakyūmu-fera* (vacuum fellatio) and *reitō-fera* (freezer fellatio). These appliance-inspired services have been growing in popularity and are also available in soaplands and urban *herusu* parlors, such as Ebisu New York II in Tokyo. In the vacuum variation, the pink hostess kneels between the customers legs and latches onto his organ. Without flagging, she begins sucking as heftily as possible. The freezer program is one of the favorite specialties at the karaoke pink salon Futago no Kyabetsu (Twin Cabbages). While the customer is singing into the microphone, the pink hostess empties a glass of ice cubes into her mouth and plunges his organ into it.

IPPŌ TSŪKO—One-Way Street
This is the basic service available in every pink salon. The hostess unzips the customer and begins rubbing him to orgasm. She might show him her breasts, but, this being a one-way service, her panties stay firmly put. Many better salons also refer to this service as their *onanii supesharu* (onanistic special).

KUROSU GĒMU—Cross Game
In this game the customer is permitted to fondle the hostess. She removes her panties, he unzips his zipper, their hands cross and they begin massaging each other until the client climaxes.

NAME-NAME PURĒ—Lick-Lick Play
Lick-lick play and lick-lick service originated in the Turkish baths in the seventies. After the customer's bath, the Turkish girls would lick him from head to foot. Today's *name-name* has been modified to accom-

modate modern tastes. The hostess licks the customer's stomach assiduously while manipulating him to a climax. In some pink salons this is also referred to punningly as *name-kuji* (slug). The woman's moist tongue passes over the customer, leaving, like the land mollusk, a slippery wet trail.

OSHIBORI SUPESHARU—Wet Towel Special

The steamed wet towels that are brought out in Japanese restaurants so that clients can refresh themselves and clean their hands before a meal, play a crucial role in genital hygiene in pink salons and other sex-trade parlors without showers. Hostesses travel from booth to booth with stacks of *oshibori*, carefully wiping the organs before and after they service them. As the *oshibori* is hot and wet, some innovative salons encourage their hostesses to use them as a sensual wrap for "onanistic" specials.

PAIZURI—Breast-urbation

Paizuri is a punning contraction of the words *oppai* (breast) and *senzuri* (masturbation). It is also known in some establishments as *paizuri zeme* (breast-urbation assault). The hostess works on the client's organ by clasping it between her breasts, which she then kneads and jolts.

An older red-light synonym popular on soapland and *herusu* menus is the poetic *tanima no shirayuri* (white lily in the valley). *Tanima* (within the valley) refers to the penile position between breasts, while *shirayuri* (white lily) is the client's sperm that ends up there after the massage. Some establishments, like Night Crew in Tokyo's Yoshiwara, offer this simply as *tanima no yuri* (the valley's lily).

A modern variation of the lily-in-the-valley program is the English *on za hiru* (on the hill). In some pink salons this is also referred to either by the amusing Anglo-Japanese name *on za hiru zeme* (on-the-hill assault) or the all-out English name *on za hiru atakku* (on-the-hill attack).

Another name that is gaining in popularity in parlors throughout Japan is *oppai-kappu* (breast-cup)—*pai-kappu* for short. The customer, "cupped" between his hostess's breasts, is brought to orgasm.

An innovative extension of "breast-urbation" is *anusu no paizuri* (anal breast-urbation). The hostess rubs lotions and creams on the customer's organ, while she stimulates his anus with her breast.

PORAROIDO SĀBISU—Polaroid Service
The hostess arrives in the dark booth with a polaroid camera. If the client pays extra, she will remove her panties, hoist her skirt, and let him take a flash photo before she services him. The customer is allowed to keep the picture as a special memento.

SAKASA TSUBO HŌSHI—Upside-Down Pot Service
The hostess removes her panties, hikes up her skirt, and planting her high heels firmly into the booth's carpet, leans back onto the sofa and exposes her "pot" to the customer. He is free to fondle her. The upside-down aspect of this service is that the usual pink protocol has the customer in a seated position with the hostess's "pot" coming down from above.

SUPOTTO-RAITO—Spotlight
The hostess brings a flashlight with her into the dark

booth, flicks on the switch and shines it under her skirt. The customer can look and touch while she is servicing him with her free hand.

TAMAKOROGASHI—Bowling

When the client announces that he would like to play bowls, he is in actual fact requesting that the pink hostess turn her attention to his testicles. *Tamakorogashi*, the Japanese word for bowling (and in some cases even roulette), literally means "ball rolling." The hostess firmly secures the client's scrotum in her mouth, and, manually massaging his organ, nimbly rolls her tongue over, under, and between the testes.

TEMAKI-ZUSHI—Hand-rolled Sushi

The customer leans back on the sofa and is approached by a pink hostess with long hair. She kneels down and wraps her tresses around his organ, much like a sushi chef would wrap the black seaweed around a role of sushi rice. Caught in her hair, the organ is then jolted to orgasm with quick repeated tugs.

TOMŌ—Net Throwing

The customer sits on the sofa in the booth with trousers and underpants round his ankles. The hostess removes her panties, and fanning her dress out over his exposed lap like a net, she sits on his knees. Slowly swaying forward and back, she massages his organ. In an illegal *honban* salon, *tomō* refers to seated intercourse.

UMANORI—Horse Riding

The hostess, facing out into the corridor away from the customer, seats herself on his organ and rides him to a climax. An equally popular but prohibited service is the *dakko-chan sābisu* (dolly service). Customer and hostess sit face to face, while he bounces her on his lap like a *dakko-chan* (little dolly).

In the clandestine *honban* salons the seated intercourse services with the hostess facing away from the client are also available as *nagenawa* (lasso) and *shiisō* (seesaw). In the lasso program she heftily rides the client's lap, like a cowboy at a rodeo show. As the excitement mounts and the bouncing becomes more unrestrained, the hostess, to keep her balance, lashes her arm through the air as if throwing a lasso.

URASUJI NAME—Rear-Muscle Lick

The customer lies back on the sofa and the pink hostess kneels between his legs. She bends forward, moves his testicles out of the way, and begins licking the sensitive zone between his scrotum and anus. She climaxes him with manual stimulation.

7 • IMAGE CLUBS

In the seventies some of the Turkish bathhouses began specializing in fancy-dress services. For years they had rubbed, washed, licked, and diddled their clients in tubs, on mats, pink chairs, and wooden horses. They had even hung their more jaded customers from ceilings in *sakasa tsuri* (upside-down suspension). The only part of the client that was not being stimulated, many felt, was his imagination, and so the bathhouses turned some of their rooms into airplane cockpits, early medieval fortress-chambers, and even girls' school classrooms.

"Imagine," the customer was told, "that you are a pilot alone in his cockpit and a stewardess enters, desperately aroused." Or, "You are the Shogun, the supreme lord of the nation, and this poor virtuous maiden in an attractive kimono is completely at your mercy." Or, what has subsequently become the most popular game on the market, "You are a teacher, your 12-year-old student was disobedient, and she must now remove her panties for disciplining."

The ploy worked. Lines of men who for years had sampled and resampled every item on the bathhouse menus energetically signed up for the new and exciting *sutorii purē sābisu* (story play service). Soon the *herusu* massage parlors got wind of the successful trend, and ordered the health girls to join in and develop their own disguises, from prison matrons to nurses.

Throughout the eighties and into the early nineties, the bathhouses, the *herusu* and *seikan* parlors, and the new S&M clubs all developed and refined their *gokko asobi* (pretend games). Such was the demand that even some of the darkest pink salons, where hostesses could be stark naked for all the customer could see, began acquiring fancy-dress wardrobes.

The parlors were proving a fashionably therapeutic outlet for the average man wishing to experiment with forbidden delicacies. If you could not afford to harass your secretary at the office, you could pop down to your local parlor for a 40-minute *sekuhara supesharu* (sexual harassment special), where you could manhandle a real secretary working on a real word processor. The more advanced customer could opt for *chikan densha* (pervert train). He could pretend he was molesting women on the subway, fondling them and even pulling their panties down. Another winner at the parlor box-offices has been *kōen de chikan* (pervert in the park). The customer prowls through an imaginary park in the dead of night and jumps a hostess disguised as a lost schoolgirl.

By 1992 the *imēji būmu* (image boom) was in full swing, bringing with it for the first time a string of specialized *imēji kurabu* (image clubs). The women at these new clubs dressed up in the outfits specified by their client, played the roles that he requested, and at "flower time," five minutes before the service was scheduled to end, would quickly massage, lick, and anally penetrate him to orgasm. The clubs were wildly successful. One of the first Tokyo clubs, Freedom in the Takadanobaba District, invented *shinkon kichin purē* (newlywed kitchen play). This image club knew that the average middle-aged customer would enjoy pretending for his 50 minutes that he had just married a girl freshly out of her teens. He enters a private room fully equipped with stove and wash basin, and the hostess discusses the various "newlywed" clothing options ranging from imported panties and bra to a full nightgown with matching curlers. Most men request the "apron—no panties" special. The hostess intones, "No sex, you must wear a condom for fellatio, anal-vibrator penetration is included in the package," and instantly changes into a happy young housewife. She is thrilled that her husband is home from work so soon, and playfully pulls him to the shower to give his organ a thorough wash and a quick check for diseases. She then playfully pulls him back into the kitchen, slips into a frilly pink apron, and energetically starts boiling water and moving pots and pans about. The client, at this point, is free to run his fingers up and down under her apron while she works. For the second half of the program, the "newlyweds" fall onto the futon, which for convenience has been placed right next to the stove. The customer is condomed, and he and the hostess move into *soixante-neuf*. Fifty minutes cost $130.

Another image club, Gold King, which opened near the port in Yokohama in January of 1993, offered a wider choice of services. The many long samurai soap operas on television had inspired among clients a vigorous interest in the "images" of the past. Gold King obliged by modeling one of its main playrooms as a film-set version of an illustrious princely chamber, and inventing the *tono-sama supesharu* (feudal lord special) at $130 for half an hour, or $170 if the client is interested in tying up and whipping the hostess, who is disguised as a princess. In the *byōin* (hospital playroom), men dress up as doctors and molest a nurse with a stethoscope, while the Arabian room is set up along the lines of a Turkish harem, and the hostess dances in bloomers and veils.

Gold King's most popular image special is *taiiku* (physical education). The customer enters a room that looks like a gym in a girls' school, fully equipped with a vaulting horse and an exercise mat. He undresses, places his clothes in a wire basket, and waits on the mat. An energetic hostess appears in pigtails and gymsuit, and leads him to the shower for the mandatory wash. When he is ready, he can position himself under the horse and peek up as she repeatedly runs and jumps. The program only lasts 30 minutes, but as with all of the Gold King specials, clients are allowed *konai hassha* (inside-mouth ejaculation).

The public's interest in bondage was growing throughout 1992, and many of the new image clubs played safe by doubling as S&M parlors. Tokyo's Hummingbird, in the Ebisu District, offered sadism and masochism, but also "pervert in the park" specials. The most notorious item on the menu is *kinshin sōkan purē* (incest play). For $150 the customer can pretend that he is being serviced by his sister or, if he prefers, his mother.

In the Meguro District nearby, Peter Pan was also making a name for itself as a trendy S&M club, with an interesting collection of image programs on the side. It invented a macabre *osōshiki supesharu* (funeral special) and added to its menu drawing cards such as "stewardess play" and "samurai drama." Another popular Tokyo S&M club, Tinkabell in the Gotanda

District, brought in a whole set of eccentric *sutōrii purē* (story play) packages. In *kyōshi to seito* (instructor and student), the client can ask a whimpering pigtailed hostess in a high school uniform to fondle his organ. In a harder variation, *kannō kyōshi purē* (carnal teacher play), he can even "force" her to fellate him.

By early 1993 the image club industry had begun to expand into the provinces. Magnates sent feelers out to towns such as Aomori, Sendai, and Kōriyama in the North and to Hiroshima and Hakata in the South, all of which had their own little bustling red-light districts. What a brand-new image club in the provinces needed in order to thrive was cut-rate real estate, a central location to which men from even the remotest villages could commute by bus or train, and, most important, nearby hotels hosting hundreds of bored businessmen on overnight trips. Specialists were flown in from Tokyo and Osaka to train local women in basic image roles, and to explain to local men the purpose and use of these fashionable establishments.

The most successful of the new provincial image clubs was Pretty Girl, which opened in the Susukino District of Sapporo. Like its chic sister-clubs in Tokyo it also dabbled in trendy bondage games, and offered special rooms labeled "prison torture chamber," "women's dormitory," and "nurse's room." One of the main courses promoted by this image club was "sexual harassment"—by now wildly popular in Tokyo clubs, but still a new and strange concept in the north. Men from all over Hokkaido drove for miles to see what it was, and would return time and again for further maltreat-the-secretary lessons. In a February, 1993 interview with the scandal sheet *Shūkan Jitsuwa*, one of the image girls, a Ms. Yuka, aired her frustration at how impossibly bad the local men were at imaging—forget bondage. She adds that the businessmen from Tokyo and Osaka, on the other hand, were astonishingly adept, both sadistically and masochistically.

Back in Tokyo, *sutorii purē* (story play) was being developed into a newer and more sophisticated *shichuēshon purē* (situation play). The club would invest top yen in creating a virtual reality setup with rooms that really looked like parks, with trees, mud, puddles, and benches and artificial moonlight that even experts could not tell from the real thing. One of the pioneers in the "situation" field was Five Doors in Tokyo's Shibuya District. It began with five situation rooms, but was so successful that it added two more. Clients interested in more imaginative stimulation could ask for a whole array of specialties. The middle-aged, longing to revitalize fond memories of the back-seat fumbling of their teens could opt, for instance, for

kā sekkusu (car sex), *kakkusu* for short. The cramped interior of the car is remarkably recreated. Another favorite at the Five Doors is the *marin-biichi* (marine beach), with amazingly real sand and sun.

The newest image clubs on the 1993 scene were the *haitekku kurabu* (the high-tech clubs) such as HTV-Kan Yokohama. The client pays $75 and then sits alone in a room in front of a large television, remote control in hand. When he flicks the switch, a young woman appears on the screen and asks him what he would like her to do. The feature of this newest of image games is that the client can see the hostess, but that she, locked up and helpless in another room, cannot see him, and has to follow every command that he barks through the intercom phone. He can tell her what to wear, what to take off, and, using his remote, can zoom his lens in when he wants to take a closer look. If the client takes a particular liking to his hostess he can request a special, but expensive, *tengai dēto* (outside date).

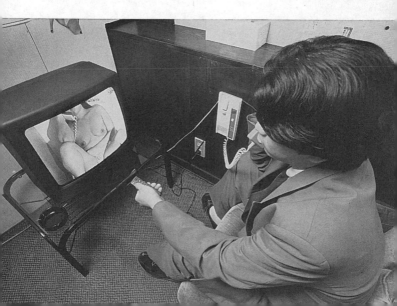

This successful marriage of the telephone to the television set caused a sensation. One of the giant electronics companies was working on successfully mass-marketing the new system, and by mid-1993 Tokyo sported 20 telephone image clubs, and Osaka 10. The idea was next snatched up in Nagoya, where three clubs opened in quick succession: I Love Telephone, 5 Cents, and Jūyaku Denwa Shitsu (Director's Telephone Room). In an interview with the popular magazine *Asahi Geinō*, Nakamoto Ryūtarō, a representative of Pioneer, declared that the aim of this TV-phone amalgam was that once the system was in full swing, masses of women could profitably provide audiovisual excitement from the comfort of their homes.

8 • THE ALL-MALE SCENE

If a Westerner should manage to barge past the No Foreigners! sign of a Japanese gay hustler bar and dash up the narrow staircase into the lounge area, he would immediately be struck by a strange sight: clients grouped on one side of the bar, drinking, singing songs, or chatting with friends, while the hustlers congregate on the other side, lined up against the wall. The elderly club manager shuffles energetically back and forth between the two groups, nodding at an old customer, whispering something to a boy, making sure that everyone is having fun, and keeping a sharp eye out for men who are ready to buy. A wink, and he's at the client's side. He quotes prices, service time, and gives a detailed rundown as to which boys do what.

Customers are divided into three distinct classes: the *sofuto-na kyaku* (soft client), the *hādo-na kyaku* (hard client), and what is known as the *urutora-hādo* (ultra-hard). Those who are "soft" like going to expensive restaurants in the company of an attractive young male, and are satisfied with an innocent kiss-and-fumble. These "easy" customers are reserved for the two or three boys whose looks and popularity have rocketed them to the top of the bar's hustler hierarchy. Most clients, however, are "hard," and expect to take their hustler to gay hotels such as the 24 Kaikan in the Asakusa District, or the Gentleman in front of the communist headquarters in Kobe City. Boys at the bottom of the spectrum are left to accommodate the hardest clients, those demanding *anaru fakku sābisu* (anal fuck service). As hustlers and clients leave the bar the manager carefully totes up the *pinhane*, the 40 percent "kickback" that the bar gets from each deal.

Many bars, like Young Mates in Tokyo and Milkland in Osaka, also offer *shutchō* (delivery). If a man is too busy or too bashful to come in person, he can check in at a gay hotel, call the bar from his room, and order a boy over the phone. The manager asks a few probing questions, "Would you prefer manual, lip, or anal?," suggests a special or two, "We now also offer S&M, dildo-deluxe, and threesomes!" and then recites the "delivery" price list: "Two hours $150, three hours $200, and all-nighters $250 even."

When the deal has been clinched, the manager whips out his pager and beeps a suitable young man from his pool of part-time hustlers that work for him out of their homes. Pioneer and King of College, the oldest working bars in Tokyo, have over a hundred boys on call, while the manager of Osaka's Date Salon has been known to beep up to 200 boys on a busy night. To ensure that customers are fully satisfied, reputable bars offer *chenji* (change). If a hustler does not meet with the client's immediate approval, he is guaranteed a replacement within 20 minutes.

Japanese hustler bars tend to stick together. Most of the newest huddle discreetly in modern high rises in districts such as Osaka's Dōyama or Hakata's Sumiyoshi, while the more blatant bars of the gay Shinjuku Ni-chōme District in Tokyo are jammed together all the way from Shinjuku Street up Nakadori.

The methods of Japan's contemporary male-hustler scene developed in the post-World War II Shinjuku. The whole area had been flattened by bombs, but within weeks of the Allied Occupation rows of black market stalls had moved in around the main station, followed by unlicensed red-light dives, shanty-taverns, and the *kasutori*-moonshine taprooms of Harmonica Alley which served liquor so potent that patrons often went blind. Along with them came the first small smoky bars with female impersonators and male hookers. The slogan of the day was "Hikari wa Shinjuku yori" or "All beams of light come from Shinjuku."

The beams of light grew even stronger after the allies left in 1952, and the first all-out male bars Yakyoku, Adonis, and Shire moved in between the brothels and the red-light groggeries of the area. Then in 1957, the Anti-Prostitution Law rubbed out the straight competition, and as one brothel after another was shut down, gay clubs, bars, salons, massage parlors, dildo stores, and restaurants set up shop. Shinjuku Ni-chōme became distinctly gay.

Throughout the sixties, bars opened by the dozen—Silk Road, Lamancha, Taboo, La Cave, Tami—almost 200 by 1970. In the 1974 spring issue of Japan's first gay magazine, *Barazoku*, in an article titled "Shinjuku Collection," journalist Mamiya Hiroshi goes on an ecstatic walking tour of Nakadori Street. Gay lib was on the rise, and for the first time men were seen walking arm in arm. Mamiya entices his reader with staggering lists of gay hotels, porn-shops, and rent-a-boy bars.

The Shinjuku gay magnates had been quick to form a tight knit, mob-like association that had become so powerful by the seventies that no one from the outside could open up a new establishment without their blessing. Even the fiercest Yakuza gangs could not penetrate the network, and the police were finding it increasingly difficult to raid the area. Soon tales were told of kindhearted drag queens courageously shielding favored criminals from the law in their impenetrable mesh of bars, clubs, and brothels.

The Japanese all-male bar finds it easier to dabble in prostitution than its heterosexual counterpart. According to Japan's penal code, even the toughest bouts of homosexual intercourse can not be defined as sex—so even when hustler money is exchanged, men cannot technically "connect their sex organs." Many of the Shinjuku District bars go further than merely providing boys for their clientele. Some of the older places, like King of College, which opened in 1977, double as brothels. When the client has chosen his hustler, the package price he pays includes a room on the premises: $135 for two hours, $155 for three, and $250 if he wishes to stay over. The manager of Pioneer , an even older "host bar" nearby, discreetly refers to this practice as *maruhi rūmu sābisu* (secret room service).

Japanese hustler bars divide themselves into three very distinct categories: "homo," "gay," and "new-half." According to modern homosexual jargon (*onē-kotoba*, "sister-language") a homo is a regular, straight-looking guy who is sexually attracted to others like himself, while a gay uses feminine language, wears dresses and makeup, and prefers sexual partners who are as straight as possible. The men from these two groups avoid each others' bars, for as the hustler-saying goes: "Homo no gei girai, gei no homo

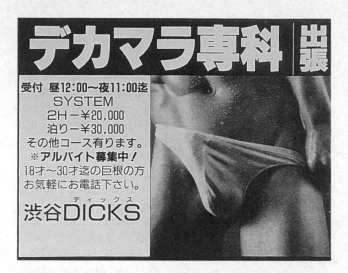

girai," or "Homos hate gays, gays hate homos." The third group, the new-half, is made up of individuals who have undergone *maki-maki* (sex-change). This final category has managed to successfully infiltrate the modern *herusu* massage scene. Expensive parlors like New Half Monogatari (New Half Legend) in Osaka service regular businessmen interested in more exotic stimulation at $180 an hour. Signs proclaim: "Our girls like it from behind."

The Japanese male-hustler industry has over the years diversified to an astonishing degree. Specialized bars, agencies, saunas, "gyms," and "tanning salons" make it their business to hire hustlers to fit the most eclectic tastes. Shibuya Dicks, for instance, specializes in only very well-endowed young men. The recruiting ads it places in gay magazines such as *Barazoku* and *Sabu* are emphatic that only men with a *kyo-kon* (gigantic root) need apply. Other Tokyo agencies, like Field and Flex, send out body builders, while Work Post is renowned for its stable of obese boys. Another important Tokyo agency, Popeye, delivers straight athletes for *sekuhara* (sexual harassment). Customers are asked over the phone how many boys they would like and whether they prefer judo, rugby, casual boys in jeans, or very young boys in high school uniforms. When the client has decided, he is given a rundown of possible underwear choices: boxer-shorts, briefs, bikinis, *ketsu-ware* ("ass-dividers" or jockstraps), or even skimpy leather thongs. Popeye hustlers arrive holding little bags in which they carry the uniform the customer has chosen. They bow, introduce themselves, and dart into the bathroom to change.

The single largest group of specialized hustling agencies caters to men in search of middle-aged and even elderly bedmates. In Tokyo, hustler services like Yasaka and After 5 send out men in their forties and fifties at $115 for one-and-half hours, and $160 for two. What makes these elderly hustlers irresistible, many feel, is their grey-haired, well-groomed look that spells executive power. While the younger hustler will pose as a high school boy, a college student, or a professional athlete, these elderly men make their entry as the venerable company chairman, or the hard-driving president who hires and fires his executives at the flick of a wrist.

Men who pay top yen to meet these mature gentlemen are known as the *fukesen zoku* (maturity-freak clique). This group has its own bars, its own pick-up joints, and its own gyms. It even has its own porn-magazines—*Samson*, *Chūnen Ai* (Middle-age Love), and *Hōman* (Plump)—which titillate the reader with nude pictures of overweight, elderly porn-stars in X-rated embraces. They also offer snippets of information like plots of new video hits such as *Monzetsu Ojiisan* (Sex-crazed Grandpa) and list names and numbers of organizations specializing in older men.

Institutions that cater to the maturity-freak gang have themselves branched out in specialized directions. The Komagome Kenkō Sentā (Komagome Health Center), for instance, in front of the Daikoku Temple in Toshimaku, is an eccentric gay gym frequented by elderly gentlemen who wish to meet other elderly gentlemen. It offers a workout area, a spa, and also private rooms in which clients can rest, even for the whole night if need be. Other places like Semishigure, an all-male soapland in Osaka, and Tompei, a massage parlor in Tokyo, target clients attracted to elderly and corpulent men who smack more of the provincial farmer than the company chairman. Miyazaki, a bar in Osaka, specializes in pudgy hosts in their forties, while Donguri in Tokyo employs only 50-year-olds and up. For a one-drink minimum, customers are permitted to fondle the host of their choice. Other Tokyo bars, like Hachan and Moto, specifically attract younger males, students, and young urban professionals, who are interested in the *oyaji taipu* (daddy type).

Many older hustlers find it more profitable to freelance without the expensive support of an agency or a bar. These groups are known on the scene as the *puro gurūpu* (pro groups). The elite pros work by referral only, whereas the discount pros can be found working out of public rest rooms in downtown districts like Shimbashi in Tokyo. These rest rooms are referred to in the trade as *hattenba* (places of development). One of the more successful Tokyo toilets is the men's room on the Ginza side of the Shimbashi Station. Regulars pop their heads in to see who is hanging out, wink, and then discreetly leave with the *puro* of their choice for a $50 spree. If there are no regulars about, the hustler stands by the urinals, patiently waiting. He keeps his eye trained on the urinating men, ready for any prospective clients to give themselves away with a rapid sidelong glance.

Hustling in these "places of development" is not a new phenomenon in Japan. In a 1977 article for *Barazoku* magazine, reporter Kimura Kenji set out on a toilet reconnaissance mission. He starts off by peeking into the men's rooms of Shimbashi Station, where he meets a heavy but attractive 50-year-old whose going price was $10 to $15 a shot. Flustered, he makes a getaway. The nervous journalist then walks a quarter of a mile towards the Ginza District, to a toilet under the Tsuchi Bridge. There is an unfortunate police box right by the toilet, and the men scuttle out every time a policeman uses the facility, but Kimura is impressed by the brisk action. He sits in his car for an hour monitoring the entrance, and notes that 13 businessmen between the ages of 30 and 50 were making full use of the facilities. The proximity of the police force, he comments, rules out the possibility of the eating of *matsutake* (mushrooms) on the premises. If caught, the offenders would be dragged to the precinct and locked up for three days for indecent exposure.

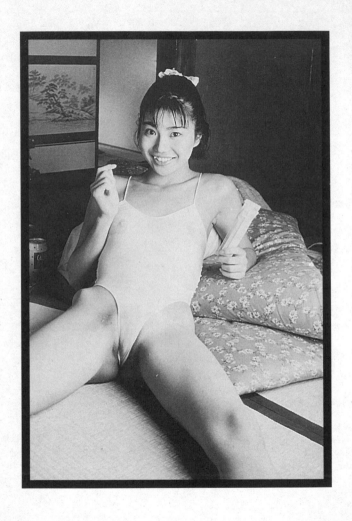

9 • THE PORN TRADE

A Western specialist plowing through the magazine racks of a Japanese sex shop is struck by the richness and the variety of the material. Shelf after shelf of enigmatic magazines classified by genre as "entangle books," "simple books," and more mysteriously "penetration issues," "shine-through editions" and "pull-between editions" are enough to convince even the most hardened foreign pornographer that the work of his Japanese counterparts displays a depth and an angle of attack unheard of at home.

"What do they have that we don't?" the Western specialist might stammer as his fingers tap frantically over the various shrink-wrapped magazine covers. "Paper quality? Lighting? Or is it the way they show every combination of men, women, and sometimes pets?"

The answer is that Japanese pornography is what it is because of a delicate interplay of historical factors, fierce competition, and, most important, stringent police surveillance that forbids the picturing of sexual organs and pubic hair. Any organs that might inadvertently appear are immediately blacked out by the authorities with either a *bokashi* (shading off), or the more sophisticated mechanical *tenkezuri* (dot gradation), a system that disgruntled pornographers have dubbed *arai* (washing).

The main mission of the modern magazine pornographer is to ensure that his reader's interest does not flag for a second or, worse, that it does not turn to the potentially more stimulating *ei bui* (AV for Adult Video, the ominous initials of the Japanese porn magazine's deadliest competitor).

With washing on one side, and this looming invasion of turf on the other, pornographic writers, cartoonists, and editors, even the magazine magnates must fight tooth and nail for their place in Japan's sex-trade world.

To keep the public titillated, pornographic photographers are constantly branching out, researching and developing ever more sophisticated techniques to show as much of a model as possible without him or her being washed by the authorities. A picture with a dot over its vital center is pornographically worthless, and is to be avoided at all cost.

So what do magazines do if they aren't allowed to show organs or even pubic hair? How can pornography exist? The answer is: evasive maneuvers. For example, one of the more successful types of magazine is the *karamibon* (entanglement book). Its specialty is attractive and sometimes star-studded pictures showing bodies male and female in any combination, entangled in passionate and often ingenious embraces. An offshoot of *karamibon*, *esu-emu karami* (S&M entanglement), for instance, might feature pictures of models in the throes of ecstasy, tied together naked, bound and gagged, hanging handcuffed upside-down from a leather chandelier. Add a dominatrix or two with a burning candle or a whip, and smear a sperm-like substance over the victims, and even a Western connoisseur might blush. The nimble camera, however, misses all the incriminating organs by a hair so that the magazine can safely hit the stands.

An even more successful sex-shop hit is the *tsukomibon* (penetration book). It specializes in women (and in certain cases men) being blatantly penetrated, or penetrating themselves with objects in such a way that the object just happens to block from view any parts that might be prone to censorship.

Another recently perfected evasion has been labeled *shiboru* (pulling between). This calls for a female model to wear a G-string or a thong-like aerobics outfit, which she artfully pulls up into her crotch. Technically this covers the offending organ, but in fact it reveals everything.

The most ingenious method of dodging censorship has been dubbed in pornographic circles *suke*, short for *sukeru* (shining through). *Suke* magazines resort to beaches, swimming pools, or jacuzzis for their backdrops, and depending on the readers' preferences show male or female models in wet (and thus transparent) swimsuits or underwear. Although absolutely everything "shines through," the organs are covered and not breaking the law.

PORNOGRAPHY—THE GOLDEN YEARS

Medieval Japanese pornographers did not have the sharp eye of the law to keep them in check. Earthy sketches, paintings, and illustrations called *makura-e* (pillow pictures) thrived, depicting intercourse from every conceivable angle. Erotica was not regarded as immoral or unethical, and was not discouraged by the state religion Shinto, or "the way of the gods." Medieval Japanese did not have the dogmatic horror of sex in art that was characteristic of their Judeo-Christian contemporaries in the West. Shinto was open, without doctrines, and regarded all natural phenomena as sacred.

Buddhism, when it arrived in Japan in the sixth century AD, brought with it Chinese and Korean artisans, temple architects, and sophisticated painting techniques that injected local erotica with new virtuosity. Out of this delicate Sino-Japanese mixture of styles the refined *shunga* (spring pictures), arose. Men and women, alone and in groups, are shown in the 48 traditional sumo wrestling positions prescribed by medieval Japanese sexologists in their illustrated sex manuals.

Unlike their modern counterparts, these early pornographic artists were free to depict genitalia, which they did with amazing gusto. They widened the fe-

male organ and lengthened and thickened the male's to grotesque dimensions. While the subject's body would be rendered in a few elegant brush strokes, a disproportionate amount of ink would be spent developing an organ's distinctive anatomical attributes. When a baffled thirteenth century student asked his venerable master, the Abbot Toba, why he was not allowed to down-scale his male organs the Abbot is reported to have snapped, "If it were drawn to natural size it would hardly be worth looking at!"

The intricacies of sex had become fashionable as early as the Asuka Period (AD 538–710), and the *osozoku no e* (posture pictures), with their in-depth analytic writing and their vivid paintings, became the rage. Eager to follow Chinese intellectual trends, the government passed the Taihō reforms in 701, which required that all doctors carefully study the illustrations of these sex manuals. As medical interest in sex grew, *shunga* artists of the Heian Period (794–1185) began to try their hand at deliberately pornographic material. This coincided with the first mass production of handscrolls, known as *emaiki-mono*, which made erotica more accessible to the refined upper-classes: the aristocracy, the powerful Buddhist clergy, and rich samurai.

One of the first pornographic works to appear in these scrolls was the notorious *Yōbutsu Kurabe* (The Penile Contest), which circulated in the late eleventh century. In it, a bored Imperial Court decides to sponsor a nationwide contest in which well-endowed men had to strip in front of a panel of judges and present their erect *yōbutsu* (shining things), to be measured. A nineteenth century copy of this scroll shows a group of young men sitting in a circle, their organs bouncing up to their chins, and in some cases even over their heads, while two gleeful judges hold out a minute measuring stick. Size, however, was not the only quality of interest to the Court; the coveted Imperial Palm could only be given to finalists whose *yōbutsu* matched their sexual endurance. A curtain is lifted and a hoard of frenzied court ladies, who had been secretly watching the measuring, rushes at the finalists. Eager for the prize, men and women throw themselves at each other, but the women display so much more endurance that they are awarded the Imperial Palm after the last male finalist collapses exhausted on the tiles.

The first real pornographic boom in Japan occurred at the beginning of the Edo Period in the early 1600s, when new methods of woodblock printing extended the *shunga* to the newly rich and very decadent merchant classes. With the boom came the first Anti-Obscenity Laws of the 1660s, which, if anything, increased the public's hunger for erotica. For the first time pornography acquired the cachet of a forbidden and possibly dangerous pleasure. Master artists like Moronobu, Sugimura, and Torii raised erotica to new heights, developing their styles in picture books, prints, and paintings. Men with women, men with men, excited voyeurs, and exquisitely balanced group scenes made high art out of the spring pictures.

Throughout the eighteenth century, artists with pornographic interests found it increasingly difficult to publish, as new edicts brought tougher restrictions. The master writer and illustrator Santō Kyoden was forced to sit at home in hand-cuffs for 50 days, while the famous painter Utamaro was thrown into prison for 50 days for "sexual innuendoes."

The first major reversal for Japanese pornography came in the late 1860s with Japan's opening to the West during the Meiji period. Impressed with sober European decorum and Victorian morality, the Meiji government plainly dealt pornography a fatal blow with its *Shuppan Jōrei* (Publishing Regulations) of 1869.

Dark days were to follow. During the next 76 years, until the invading allies disbanded the government censorship bureau in 1945, 4,505 books were banned along with tens of thousands of newspapers, magazines, and pamphlets. All pornography, from refined *shunga* to pinups, went underground and was available only as an expensive and dangerous black-market delicacy. The most notorious sex press of the Taishō Period (1912–1926) was *Ero-guro Bunko*, short for "erotic-grotesque library." Braving prison sentences and fines, it brought out such progressive bestselling titles as *Dansā to Zurōsu* (The Danseuse and Her Bloomers), *Ushimusume ni Namerareta Hanashi* (I Was Licked by a Cowgirl), and *Hadaka no Shoppu-gāru* (The Naked Salesgirl), until they too were suppressed in 1930.

But while the government hounded pornography and arrested its creators, its distributors, and its readers, it was not above producing its own hard-core material when it needed to. During the 1904 war with Russia the Japanese soldiers at the front were thunderstruck when shipload upon shipload of military mail began arriving chock-full of some of the lewdest postcards they had ever seen—all with the official *gunji yūbin* (military mail) stamps on the back. The Imperial Army's morale could under no circumstances be allowed to flag. Under the motto "All's fair in love and war," the Japanese government and the armed forces had commissioned cards on which girls were squatting, bending over, lying down, and revealing everything, with angles and poses that were progressive even by Western standards of the day. Every time a major offensive was planned, more explicit photos arrived, some of them even of European origin for soldiers with an interest in Caucasian girls.

But the idea of pornography for the forces had not been thought up as only a morale booster. It was remembered that a decade earlier, during the Sino-Japanese war of 1894, whole platoons of soldiers had returned to Japan infected with venereal disease. Erotic postcards, it was hoped, would keep soldiers from succumbing.

By the 1890s, a military postal network had been set up to handle a one-way flow of mail from the soldiers abroad to Japan, and when the service was upgraded to a two-way flow early in the twentieth century, some of the first material to travel to the front was pornography. Certain factions of the army and the government, however, were outraged, and the official "Porn for the Boys" movement came to a definitive end with Japan's victory in the Russo-Japanese war. Neither the government nor the army ever dabbled in pornography again or ever admitted that they had.

Most of the photo-postcards produced during the government's two-year pornographic spree ended up for sale on Japan's black market. Some of the naughtier Taishō Period geisha handed them out to their favorite customers as presents.

THE BIRTH OF MODERN PORNOGRAPHY

Modern pornography was born in 1945 when the allies obliterated the old censorship bureau. Hundreds of magazines sprang up over night, feeding the devastated and hungry masses with humorous and erotic stories, cartoons, and escapist fantasies. The populace became addicted and soon these imprints were given the nickname *kasutori*, from the rough and highly alcoholic moonshine liquor *kasutori shochu* to which more and more people were turning in desperation. These *kasutori* magazines were the first to dare experiment openly with nude covers, explicit illustrations, and risqué texts.

To survive in tough post-war Japan the *kasutori* publisher had to have his wits about him. He had to be street-smart, affable with the right people, and most important a master at networking and connection-pulling. To keep his magazine going he needed more than a good editorial staff, resourceful reporters, sharp cartoonists, and witty fiction writers who knew when to describe a kiss, a cuddle, or a heroine's kimono falling open to reveal a passionate knee. Even though readers were hungry for *kasutori* and would buy up any copies they could find, a publishing house had to overcome many obstacles before its magazine could safely find its way into readers' hands.

The biggest feat of all was to get the magazine printed. Ink, fuel, and especially paper were practically unobtainable from 1945 to 1950, and a magazine publisher would have to spend most of his time trying, by foul means or fair, to get his hands on some. To do so he would have to keep a strict and detailed social calendar, wining and dining paper-factory magnates, officials in charge of paper-rationing coupons, Yakuza moguls who controlled black-market paper supplies, and gang bosses who dealt in paper delivery. When all else failed, publishers were even known to go on extended field trips deep into the provinces in search of bark, pulp, and fuel, which they would then deliver personally to paper factories.

Once the publisher had enough paper to meet his circulation quota, the real work started. In an age where photographs of nude women were out of the question, the successful porn magazine had to secure the services of freelance superstar cartoonists like Ono Saseo and the controversial Yokoyama Taizō, whose frisky sex-cartoons (never more than a feminine breast or two showing) were always a hit.

Once the magazine was off the press, the next hurdle was to sneak the offending material past Article 175 of Japan's Criminal Code, with which the government, despite the demise of the censorship bureau, could still lucratively pounce on "obscene literature." This evasion was the hardest part, as the authorities, in spite of the more than half a million prostitutes, the countless pimps, and more than a million amphetamine freaks and heroin addicts stalking Japan's streets, were determined to keep magazine readers as pure as possible.

Before World War II, magazines had to pass through the tight net of the censorship laws which the Allies replaced with their own Occupation Press Code, designed to eliminate unpropitious political material.

The occupiers, however, were not particularly interested in monitoring girlie magazines. Busy elsewhere, the general headquarters left control of obscenity in the hands of the overworked police force. The postwar years, the pornographers believed, would be an era in which all could be bared. In October of 1948 the magazine *Toppu* (Top) featured a realistic painting of a topless young woman on its cover, while *Beze* (from the French *baiser*, "kiss") dared to run a cartoon of a young couple surprised by an earthquake while frolicking naked in a large construction pipe. (But the delighted public did not get to see much, since both characters happened to be clutching at their clothes as they were escaping from the pipe).

The porn press was poised to make a killing from the new sexual franchise when the police department decided to shape up and crack down. Publishers suddenly found themselves in a catch-22 situation. Article 175 of the 1907 Revised Criminal Code was (and remains) dangerously vague. "A person," it proclaims, "who distributes or sells obscene writing, pictures or other objects, or who publicly displays them, will be punished with imprisonment at forced labor for not more than two years, or will be fined not more than ¥5,000 (the amount is to be revised in proportion to inflation) or with a minor fine. The same applies to individuals who possess the above with the intention of selling."

With the police left to their own anti-pornographic devices, rough times were ahead.

The great purge began when the December, 1946 issue of *Ryooki* (Bizarreness Hunt) published "H. Taisa Fujin," (Colonel H.'s wife). It was a vignette by Kitagawa Chiyozō in which a young woman allowed herself to be seduced by a 19-year-old student while her soldier husband was away teaching villagers guerrilla warfare. The immorality and effrontery of a woman straying while her husband was away fighting for Emperor and country was more than the criminal courts could digest. With the story's risqué plot and intriguing title the magazine became a best seller, even at the exorbitant price of ¥12. The story gave few details, but enough was hinted at to drive readers of the time into a sexual frenzy. The narrator, a teenage student, falls in love with the wife of a home-guard captain at whose house he is staying. One day, hearing strange moaning sounds in the bathroom, he peeks through the window and sees the frenzied couple entangled in the tub. The innocent boy dwells on the interesting interplay of the soldier's dark hue and the alabaster-like translucence of the woman's skin. Filled with desire, he hankers after the woman night and day. She notices his attentions and engages in the type of soft-porn banter that, as the Osaka writer Fujimoto Giichi comments in his essay "Kanki Kanki" (Delight Delight), was enough to make postwar readers play with themselves frenetically.

"You are still young . . . I guess you wouldn't know how to . . . " she tells the student.

"What do you mean?"

"Oh, nothing."

"I'm 19! I'm a grown man!"

"But if your parents found out, they'd be furious."

The young woman invites the narrator to take a bath with her. While they slowly wash each other she utters the fatal words that started the 1947 purge, "Anata no mono wa rippa da ne!" (Ooh, you have a nice one there!)

Ryooki was fined heavily and the police went on a confiscation spree, targeting outlets throughout major urban centers. The diligent officers managed to seize 873 copies, but not before the magazine cashed in a record profit of nearly one and a quarter million yen. A substantial number of copies reached the black market, where their price was marked up from ¥12 to ¥150. Within a few days the rival *kasutori* magazine *Dekameron* was attacked by the censors, and a few weeks later, before the porn crowd got over this double shock, the magazine *Sei Bunka* (Sex Culture) was caught, followed closely by *Danran* (Relaxation) and *Suriru* (Thrill), a light political magazine that had an immaculate record until it tried to whip up its circulation with a topless girl on its cover.

Between 1947 and 1949 over 120 *kasutori* magazines were charged with obscenity. Lifelike cover illustrations, forbidden vocabulary, and even cartoons fell victim to the police. *Kyoen* (Strange Lust), for instance, was raided for printing words like *nozurōsu* ("bloomer-less" or ladies without underwear), and seductive Latin medical terms like *koitasu* (coitus), *onanisumu* (onanism), and a misspelled *orugasumu* (it should have been *orugazumu* for "orgasm"), while the magazine *Ryooki*, under its new name *Ryōki Zeminaru* was zapped again in 1948 for a candid exposé of the latest red-light craze—striptease.

Each additional scandal fired up the public's lust for more porn. The larger the fine, the greater the sales. Even when prices doubled, tripled, and quadrupled and the paper became so brittle that readers often had to guess at the smudgy text, magazine sales kept rising. In a recent essay, Nosaka Akiyuki, the prize-winning author of *The Pornographers*, comments on the amazing fact that even though the government had passed an emergency law in 1945 that limited all income to an average of ¥600 a month, the frantic public still snatched up magazines at ¥20 to ¥30 apiece. He remembers with a pang that as an excited but poor 15-year-old he was reduced to buying ten yen *kasutori* fakes, collaged together at random from old issues, until luck brought him in contact with a black-market distributor of outlawed hard-core magazines like *Futon Nōto* (Futon Notebook), which he was allowed to rent at ten yen a shot.

The prize-winning novelist, Fujimoto Giichi (host of the spicy TV sex show *11p.m.*), fared better. In his article "Delight Delight" he confesses that as he was in the habit of stealing G.I. weapons at a profit of ¥5,000 each, he had unlimited access to magazines. He remembers the sexual fervor with which he leafed through his first *kasutori*, which had a Rodin sculpture on the front and the title "Delight Delight" on the back, underneath which was a woodblock print of a naked girl at a spa, squatting over a jet of water, feverishly washing herself.

Just as the sex and the obscenity scandals of early 1947 were whipping readers' enthusiasm to new heights, everyone, including the black market, ran out of paper. In frantic desperation, successful new mega-magazines like *Hāto* (Heart), *Sei Bunka* (Sex Culture), *Raburii* (Lovely), and *Aka to Kuro* (Red and Black) turned to *senkashi*, a crude type of toilet paper.

The public, hungry for titillation, bought on. New *kasutori* sprang up overnight, lasted for two or three issues, were cornered by the police, and disappeared, only to reappear under new names. Popular opinion had it that just as three shots of *kasutori* moonshine

could down the hardiest drinker, the hardiest publishers were inevitably downed after their third *kasutori*
magazine.

With the end of the Allied Occupation in the early
fifties, the frenzied *kasutori* era began sizzling out.
Japan's postwar nightmare was drawing to a close,
and the mentality of "publish, grab the money, run"
was no longer financially feasible. The public still had
the "hots," but pornographers were beginning to
totter under the expensive strain of constant police
raids, fines, and arrests. There were now clear signs
that Japan was rising from the ashes, and even the
most swashbuckling magazines began to crave some
semblance of stability.

There had been a sigh of relief in 1947, when
Article 21 of the new constitution proclaimed, "no
censorship shall be maintained." But as the subsequent shower of arrests was to prove, this gigantic
step towards freedom of speech did not include pornographic speech. The times called for a newer, safer
approach to obscenity, and the magazines busied
themselves with new techniques.

The first was humor. How gamy could you get
before you were dragged off in handcuffs? Uncouth
vignettes started appearing alongside frolicking line
drawings. A pervert, arrested, confesses that he is
driven to harass young girls out of sheer desperation—his wife devours so many onions "that even her
pussy smells of them." The magazine survived the
anecdote, and a hotter story was launched. An ex-
general is being held captive for war crimes. His
interviewer, aware of the captive's tastes, asks him,
"Do you eat pussy?" The General is so outraged that
he slips, "Oh come on! Do you think I would lick

anything that salty?" The police were not amused, and formally warned the star cartoonist Yokoyama Taizō that if he didn't tone down his humorous illustrations he would be arrested.

As magazines scuttled about looking for new profitable but pragmatic approaches to obscenity, *Hanashi* (Stories) came up with a solution that was to redirect the path of porn for decades to come. Japan was being rebuilt and modernized, and the government was eagerly trying to educate the masses, to expose them to modern, Western ideas. If official campaigns could deal with sticky subjects like birth control and safe sex, *Hanashi* argued, why shouldn't a popular magazine help the government enlighten the hundreds of thousands of eager readers. The pornographic scene was amazed that *Hanashi*, of all magazines, should hit the jackpot. It had been around since 1933, published by the prestigious Bungei Shunjūsha and was something of a joke among the hard-core crowd because of its maudlin editorial policy. But in 1948 it changed its name to *Fūfu Seikatsu* (Family Life) and rocketed to best-sellerdom with enlightening articles like "Wafū no Toire no Naka de Seikō Suru Hōhō," (How to have sex in a Japanese-style toilet).

By June, 1949 *Fūfu Seikatsu*, the last of the *kasutori* giants, was Japan's number one seller. Competing magazines, hungry for action, started copying its name and style. Over the next few years a flood of variations spilled onto the scene, among them *Fūfu to Seikatsu* (Family and Life), *Modan Fūfu Seikatsu* (Modern Family Life), *Modan Seikatsu* (Modern life), *Fūfu Sekkai* (Family World), and *Fūfu Zasshi* (Family Magazine). In 1954, the peak of the *fūfu* craze, over ten new "family" magazines popped up.

In 1950 the premiere issue of *Ningen Tankyū* (Human Research) became a *succes de scandale* by going beyond "family planning" and launching its pornographic stories under the banner of serious scientific research. It was the man in the street, however, and not the biologist, who was meant to be seduced by bouncy articles like "Orugasumu no Hyōjo," (All about orgasm), and "Shakai Mondai to Sei," (Social problems and sex). The following year *Amatoria* usurped the top slot to be supplanted in 1953 by the even bolder *Fuzoku Kagaku* (Sexual Science). By 1957 an amazed Supreme Court decided that free speech was fine and good, but there had to be limits. Too many youngsters were reading these magazines, it was thought, and as a result were becoming delinquents, and the late fifties and early sixties saw a rush of societies like "Kodomo o Mamoru Kai" (Protect the Children Society) and "Akusho Tsuihō" (Ban Harmful Books).

The fines, the court cases, the arrests and prison sentences of the fifties and sixties made it clear to the pornographer of the seventies that the police were not going to relax their pubic hair guidelines. However nude a model might be, not a hint of her *hea* (hair), was going to be tolerated. As a reminder that obscenity would remain as illegal as ever, four racy books on medieval Japan were immediately banned as the new decade began, among them the colorful *Edo Jidai no Seiseikatsu* (Sex Life in the Edo Period).

As the seventies unfolded the police force spent more and more time having to pore through pornography. Every risqué photograph, every explicit illustration had to be scrutinized and discussed. The workload tripled, quadrupled, and quintupled as shiploads of foreign material started pouring into the Yokohama Customs House in 1969 (growing to 48,000 questionable volumes by 1972 and 78,000 the next year). The teenagers, college girls and boys, and pensioners hired by the customs offices had to black out hundreds of thousands of organs. Spot checks had to be made at adult book shops throughout Japan to see that only above-board material was being sold, especially when word spread from pornography salesmen to readers that the censor's ink could be erased with paint thinner.

Then in 1975 lightning struck from an unexpected quarter. *Josei Jishin* (Woman's Self), a quiet magazine intended for the with-it urban housewife, did a feature subtitled "Sawareru Otoko-tachi" (Men you would like to touch). Most of the touchable men were naked Japanese models, with a four-page special on male nudes from foreign women's magazines. Organs, of course, were carefully rubbed out with delicate gradations, but more than ten men displayed an ample portion of *chimō* (male pubic hair).

The police force was at a loss. Lusty, catchy titles like "See it? Saw it? Had enough! C'mon . . . it's cool!," or "Five overseas women's magazines show penises," promised tantalizing revelations. But were naked men tantalizing? Interdepartmental memos were sent and emergency meetings were convened and everyone agreed that female pubic hair was exciting and thus illegal, but surely nobody could possibly be stimulated by a man's pubic region?

While the police squabbled among themselves the magazine hit the stalls, and a stampede of eager readers ensued. Within minutes the phones at headquarters were ringing off the hook with magazines frantically checking if they too could do profitable naked-men specials. Were naked men legal? How naked could you get before you were arrested? If showing the male pubic region was permissible, how much of the penis could be exposed and how much of the testicles? More emergency meetings. To add to the problem, the gay magazine *Barazoku* (Rose Gang), inspired by *Josei Jishin's* success, did its own pubic special in its February 12 issue, and having gotten away with it launched on an even bolder spree of naked men in April. With the controversy showing signs of becoming dangerous, Hirano Takehiro, the chief publisher of *Josei Jishin*, made a public announcement that he and his magazine had no interest in displaying naked men in the future, and that the January special had been intended merely as a playful disclosure of trends in Western magazines.

In the meantime, outraged associations of housewives were taking up arms, followed by various Parent-Teacher Organizations, all demanding that the police intercept immediately all copies of *Josei Jishin*. Overwhelmed by the dimensions the scandal was assuming, the police set about questioning women as to whether they were aroused by men's pubic hair in any way. The conclusion they came to was that as men and women were equal, so was the illegality of their pubic hair, and court dates were set to try the editors and the Japanese models.

By March, the scandal had expanded into international diplomatic quarters. The Tokyo Kokuritsu Kindai Bijutsukan (Tokyo Museum of Modern Art) launched an exhibit of some of the more explicit works of the Belgian painter Paul Delveaux. The paintings of the internationally acclaimed artist arrived safely and moved smoothly through the customs house—art, after all, even when depicting organs and pubic hair, is not pornography. The giant Japanese newspaper organization *Mainichi Shimbunsha* was co-sponsoring the exhibit and had undertaken to publish a deluxe catalogue. When the senior editors saw the surprisingly candid paintings that they were supposed to print and distribute throughout Japan, they panicked. If the *Josei Jishin* editors and even the poor male models, 16 souls in all, were about to be thrown in irons for showing a bit of male pubic hair, what would *Mainichi*'s fate be if it showed everything? So *Mainichi* decided to play safe, and printed the catalogue with dots and gradations over anything that might possibly offend Anti-Pornographic Article 175 of the Penal Code. The art critics, the intelligentsia, and the international community were outraged. Discussions about art, censorship, and freedom of speech were initiated, and when the Belgian Embassy finally threatened Japan with international ridicule *Mainichi* was forced to call back all its censored catalogues and publish a new, pristine edition.

While the *Mainichi* scandal was being sorted out at the highest levels, the public held its breath wondering what would happen to the hapless "men you would like to touch." On April 17 the court decided that the *Josei Jishin* article was really not that pornographic, and in a triumph for democracy the 16 indicted individuals were set free, as was the art director of the gay magazine *Barazoku*.

A warning was issued, however, that in the future pubic hair, whether male or female, would be considered gender-equal under the law. Future transgressions would not be tolerated.

FROM PINK CASSETTES TO POCKET PORN

The late sixties and early seventies saw pornography boldly conquer new markets. It had showed up in magazines, in picture collections, on film, live on stage—so why not, as enterprising pornographers asked themselves, offer it on audio-tapes as well? In 1968 a Kyoto recording studio, known for its snappy commercials, released its own special *pinku kasetto* (pink cassette), which offered the listener a varied selection of moaning male and female voices. A cassette, it was believed, that could conjure up vivid orgasms in stereo without having to rely on a single offending visual image, would open up a whole new pornographic frontier.

The marketing strategy was to target drivers commuting to and from work, who might enjoy some stimulation in the privacy of their own car. As automobile cassette tape decks were the newest thing, the *pinku kasetto* would inevitably turn into a gold-mine. The tapes slipped past the watchful eye of the police, and were soon clogging the shelves of auto supply stores and provincial gas stations from Kansai to Fukui.

It was not until a year later that the police in the province of Shiga, alerted by a scandalized housewife, took a closer look at the pink cassettes. The commissioner was outraged and immediately set out with his men raiding gas stations, collecting as many of the offending tapes as he could find. He arrested 19 attendants.

But was this pink cassette pornography? You couldn't see anything, the attendants argued, and anyway, they had stocked the tapes in good faith.

The police were confused—there was no precedent about how to deal with audio-porn. The 19 gas station attendants were sent home with a warning, and a police team went on a reconnaissance mission to the recording studios in Kyoto. In a process that lasted two years the police rounded up six individuals, among them the actors who had moaned for the tapes, and brought them before the courts.

The defendants pleaded innocent on the grounds that during the recording sessions the actors had been fully dressed, had sat at opposite ends of the room, and had merely given a theatrical rendition of a romantic encounter into the microphone. The judge was not quite convinced, but let them off with two years' probation. The cassette, he determined, was definitely pornographic, for it encouraged lewd thoughts, and he ruled that future tapes of this nature would not be let off so lightly. Thwarted, the budding sex-cassette industry went underground.

Before the dust had settled on the pink cassette case, the police were alerted by another indignant housewife about a far graver evil: pornographic vending machines. It was a known fact that these street-corner *jidō hambaiki* dispensed softly pornographic popular fiction, but what were ¥100 hard-core titles like *Poketto Poruno* (Pocket Porn) doing there?

Poketto Poruno was a pictorial introduction to unusual sexual positions, in the form of a self-help manual. As the Association of Tokyo Housewives pointed out, any ten-year-old with a ¥100 coin could punch the *Poketto Poruno* button. The vending ma-

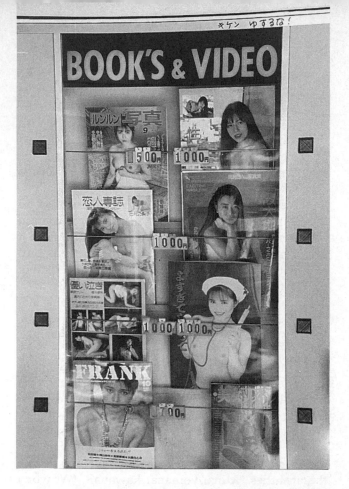

chine was seized, and the four individuals responsible for the publication were dragged off to court. To the chagrin of the police, the 1973 verdict was "innocent," for *Poketto Poruno*, it turned out, was remarkably similar to two earlier books, *How To Sex I* and *II*, which had somehow slipped past the censor.

The police went on watching and waiting by the vending machines. In August, 1971, *Modern Petting* by Matsukubo Kōhei, appeared, closely followed by another of his works, *Oral Sex* (subtitled *Kuchibiru ni yoru pettingu*, or "Petting with your lips"). When the same author came out in December of that year with a third vending machine best-seller, *Mood Sex*, followed by the even more daring and popular *Home Sex*, the police arrested both him and his publisher, Suruga Daishobo.

Nevertheless, pornographic entrepreneurs had hit the jackpot with these vending machines. You could get a basic machine for as little as ¥400,000 (the fancier urban models going for about twice that amount) and, with the monthly "foundation-fee" at a trifling ¥6,000, the stream of cash was guaranteed. By 1977, Japan boasted of more than 13,000 pornographic machines, 2,800 of them in Tokyo and 1,100 in Osaka, that dispensed over 160 pornographic magazines, many of them not available in regular stores.

As more street-corners were invaded by the porn machines and more adolescents dropped their pocket money into them, the housewives and their associations became increasingly militant. These women's groups, labeled by the pornographers as *obāsan zoku* (auntie gangs) jumped into action. The slogan that they had chanted frenetically at their meetings during the late fifties, "Minai, yomanai, kawanai!" (We won't look at it, we won't read it, we won't buy it), was supplanted by the even more ominous "Urasenai, tsukurasenai!" (We won't let you sell it, we won't let you make it). It was becoming increasingly clear in pornographic circles that it was these women, and not the police, who were truly dangerous. The Saitama City Parent-Teacher Association alone, managed to wrench the number of *jidō hambaiki* in Ikuta down from 23 machines in 1976 to a mere three in 1978.

The vending machine magnates quickly panicked. Fifteen machine associations and 20 risqué booksellers hurriedly joined forces to form the Jihankyō, an abbreviation of the National Assembly of Magazine Vending Machine Associations. Its mission was to set up its own restrictive regulations and swiftly, before the wrathful housewives gained any more ground.

The magnates convened on November 20, 1976, and invited two high-ranking police officers to give their first meeting a touch of formality. They agreed that the machines would carry a "For 18-year-olds and over" label, and that all glass panels through which the enticing magazine covers showed were to be removed. Distorting glass would have to be installed, through which only the trained eye of an adult connoisseur could detect the publication of choice. Within two days, however, before the *jidō hambaiki* machines could be modified, the Tokyo police indicted eight companies and 22 pornographers on charges of obscenity, and towed eight Tokyo vending machines out of the city. Magnates complained, pleaded, and threatened. One desperate magnate, on December 18th, even stormed into the Police Commissioner's office, pleaded innocent, and swore he would henceforth dedicate himself wholeheartedly to community service. But the "auntie gangs" were winning. By January, 1977 they cornered the first local governments in Tochigi and Nara into taking cautious anti-vending machine measures, and by May they had muscled Japan's Congress into passing the first nationwide regulations.

TEEN PORNOGRAPHY

One of the most interesting phenomena in contemporary Japanese pornography is its presence on the teenage magazine scene. Notorious publications like *Sukora* (Scholar), *Bideo Boi* (Video Boy), and *Nyan 2 Kurabu* (Meow 2 club) target high school boys, while the rollicking and harder-core *Poppu Tein* (Pop Teen) *Pasuteru Tein* (Pastel Teen) and *Puchi Seben* (Petite Seven) are meant for 10- to 13-year-old girls. These magazines use all the Anti-Porn Law evasion tricks perfected since 1945 to keep their readers turned on and buying.

The schoolboy magazines feature page after page of naked *ona-petto* (jerk-off pets), revealing the maximum amount of anatomy short of attracting the police. The ploy used by these magazines, especially by *Sukora*, is that their editorial policy is one of education and enlightenment; a healthy teen is an informed teen. And the information served up is copious: sex extravaganzas with illustrations and how-to pictures, articles on where to find the hottest pick-up action in town, what drugs are in or out and where to find them at what price. *Sukora's* scholarly titles, like "Sekai no Taii" (Body positions of the world) and "Sekkusu no Kihon no Daijiten" (An encyclopedia of the fundamentals of sex), have been especially successful. Passionate models, naked except for ribbons and exotic jewelry, demonstrate sexual positions from all over the world.

Among many acrobatic sexual stunts, *Sukora* offers its readers Chinese delicacies such as *kitō* (soaring turtle), in which the girl lies on her back waving her legs in the air while the male model approaches her from behind and between her thighs, and *sanshunrō* (three autumn puppies). *Sanshunrō* is an unlikely position in which both models lie bottom to bottom on their backs, their legs up high, with the writer expressing his skepticism about the feasibility of a boy pressing his penis down between his legs so that it can reach the girl.

For the young reader who is more adventurous the Chinese section offers *ransōbu* (dancing horse-bells), in which two girls lie on each other while their friend inserts his organ into them alternately with consecutive jabs, and *konkeirinjō* (moving the chicken), where the girl sits on the boy's penis, while a friend of hers helps her move up and down on it. For schoolboys burdened with an uncommonly large girlfriend, the magazine suggests *hōshōsū* (the king and his boy), where the reader, in this case the king, lies helplessly on the mat with the large girl squatting on his organ, while a close friend of his heaves her up and down.

As the teenager reads on the positions offered become increasingly outlandish, dangerous, and dubious. From America, the magazine features the reputedly popular "Casino Bridge" in which chairs play a vital role, and a highly improbable position called "Active Insert Herself."

Another magazine, *Tōkō Dokkiri Shashin* (Surprise Pictures by Mail), has a popular section that offers the newest and zaniest "play-with-yourself" ideas. Some are pretty basic, suggesting, for instance, that the teen approaching climax spiral his organ like a corkscrew and then let it go, bouncing into orgasm. On other occasions the magazine, at a loss for new ideas, has resorted to desperate measures, such as the bestiality article which appalled even the openminded scandal sheet *SPA*. Youths in search of the ultimate are urged to dip their organs in butter and arrange for a snake (preferably defanged) to flick away.

Another favorite magazine, *Bideo Boi* (Video Boy), educates, advises, and guides its young readers through the complex maze of the triple-X video world.

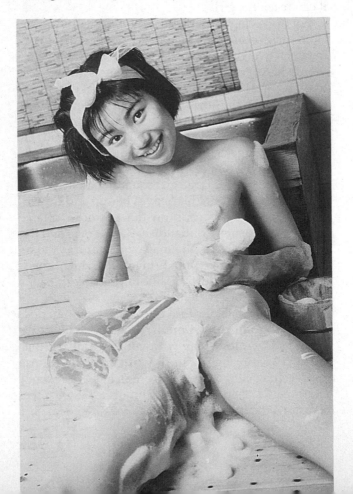

Where should a nimble schoolboy do his bargain shopping? Who are the hottest actresses on the scene, and who aren't? Where can he find the illegal, hard-core stuff? Advanced readers can even try their hand at the monthly video quiz. A panel of eight naked and promising new porn actresses are displayed in the "Bideo Aidoru Dābi" (Video idol derby). The sharp teenager who predicts which of the women will be nominated as the most talented star of the month is sent a discreetly packaged triple-X video of his choice.

The circulation of these magazines has grown steadily as the progressively steamier articles attract new readers from older age groups, especially from the *rorikon zoku* (Lolita-complex gang), made up of older men interested in teenage girls. This mature "gang" does not stop at teen boy magazines full of naked nymphets and sex telephone numbers, but also devours schoolgirl magazines. These contain lusty confessions and remarkable letters to the editor sent in by precocious little girls working with topics like sex positions, novel ideas for self-stimulation and incest, and homosexual techniques, all with a vigor that, to quote Hoshii (*Sex in Ethics and Law*), is "too provocative even for adults."

Readers quickly leaf to their favorite section, say *Pop Teen*'s "Bājin Rengō" (Virgin League), and devour articles on how to prepare a dish that smells like a *shojo no asoko* or "virgin's thing" (empty a packet of Chii-Tosu, "Cheese Doodles," into a bowl, add vinegar and let soak for three minutes), along with letters like the one in which a schoolgirl boasted that her girlfriend had massaged herself with first one drumstick, then two, then three, and is now so jaded that she cannot climax unless she is using at least five.

One of the most popular sections in *Pop Teen*'s sister magazine, *Pastel Teen*, is the prepubescent confession section. Staple features like "Onii-chan to Etchi Shichatta," (I did it with my brother), and "Watashi Etchi Daisuki—Rezu to Esu-emu Mō Kyōmi Aru" (I really like raunch—I'm also into lesbian stuff and S&M), accompanied by frank pictures submitted by less inhibited readers, guarantee when the magazine hits the streets on the seventh of every month there will be a stampede.

```
パンティー一昼夜使用・・・・・・・・・・¥ 3500
  〃   二昼夜使用・・・・・・・・・・・¥ 3500
  〃   三昼夜使用・・・・・・・・・・・¥ 3500
  〃   オシッコ付・・・・・・・・・・・¥ 3500
  〃   ウンコ付・・・・・・・・・・・・¥ 4000
  〃   特選品・・・・・・・・・・・・・¥ 5000
生理パンティー・・・・・・・・・・・・・・¥ 3500
小学生使用パンティー・・・・・・・・・・・¥ 3500
中学生使用パンティー・・・・・・・・・・・¥ 3500
高校生使用パンティー・・・・・・・・・・・¥ 3500
女子大生使用パンティー・・・・・・・・・・¥ 3500
お楽しみ三点セット・・・・・・・・・・・・¥ 5000
  〃   四点セット・・・・・・・・・・・¥ 7000
  〃   十点セット・・・・・・・・・・・¥14000
  〃   ランチセット・・・・・・・・・・¥ 7000
   1～7と11～15の商品に生写真付
ブラジャー・・・・・・・・・・・・・・・・¥ 2000～
ガードル・・・・・・・・・・・・・・・・・¥ 3000～
スリップ・・・・・・・・・・・・・・・・・¥ 3000～
パンスト・・・・・・・・・・・・・・・・・¥ 2000～
ボディスーツ・・・・・・・・・・・・・・・¥10000～
レオタード・・・・・・・・・・・・・・・・¥ 7000～
スパッツ・・・・・・・・・・・・・・・・・¥ 6000～
特選水着・・・・・・・・・・・・・・・・・¥ 6000～
特選ネグリジェ・・・・・・・・・・・・・・¥ 5000～
   16～24の商品に生写真付
カラーナース服・・・・・・・・・・・・・・¥10000～
看護婦白衣・・・・・・・・・・・・・・・・¥10000～
ナース服有名病院各種・・・・・・・・・・・¥10000～
セーラー服夏上下・・・・・・・・・・・・・¥ 8000～
セーラー服冬上下・・・・・・・・・・・・・¥ 8000～
セーラー夏冬上のみ・・・・・・・・・・・・¥ 5000～
セーラー服有名校各種・・・・・・・・・・・¥30000～
ブルマー・・・・・・・・・・・・・・・・・¥ 3000～
カラーブルマー・・・・・・・・・・・・・・¥ 3000～
ラインブルマー・・・・・・・・・・・・・・¥ 3000～
体操着・テニスウエアー・・・・・・・・・・¥ 7000～
スクール水着各種・・・・・・・・・・・・・¥ 3000～
```

10 • THE PANTY CONNECTION

One of the major side effects of the Meiji Restoration in the late nineteenth century was a cascade of undergarments. For centuries the kimono wearer had been panty-free, but now that Japan was open to the West, women enthusiastically embraced the radical new concept of silky and frilly undergarments.

By the 1920s, the *mo-ga* (modern gals) of the period had become addicted, and their urbane closets quickly filled with bloomers, corsets, suspenders, garters, girdles, and hose-clips. Come washday, the exotic garments would hang from windows, in yards and gardens, and from clotheslines on new Western-style balconies. Soon randy groups of *mo-bo* (modern boys) were risking their lives on drainpipes and high fences to steal them. Housewives hung their expensive bloomers higher and higher, but the *shitagi dorobō* (undergarment thief) was here to stay.

Throughout the 1930s and 1940s, as skirts grew shorter and underwear tighter, bloomers mysteriously vanished from clotheslines at an alarming pace. The older the bloomer the quicker it disappeared. Even during the war years, when a French garter cost over a month's rent and women would guard their lingerie with their lives, the *zurōsu-dorobō* (bloomer thieves), as they were known at the time, were insatiable.

The decades passed, miniskirts came and went and came again, and the tastes of the *shitagi-mania zoku* (panty-freak gang) became ever more refined. Many felt that the washed and tumbled panty on the clothesline just didn't offer the stimulation of the unwashed article. But how was one to secure such an item? Breaking and entering into apartments was one option, *itabashiri* (locker-room thieving) was another. But risking one's life on a precarious balcony railing was not everyone's cup of tea, and many panty-aesthetes, among them well-to-do businessmen, company chairmen, and crotchety patriarchs, could not afford to be seen climbing garden fences. By the late sixties, well-organized underground networks appeared that provided heavily soiled panties under the counter for exorbitant prices.

When the panty-specialist Ikeda Kunihiro opened his second-hand undergarment boutique, Mikki, in Ōmiya City, there was a stampede. In short order not a panty was left on the shelves. Customers were banging down the door, phones rang off the hook, and bulk orders flooded in. Ikeda hastily placed emergency ads in women's magazines: "Boutique seeks used panties—minimum three-day usage a must." Within days, high school girls, secretaries, young housewives, and mature matriarchs wheeled in cartloads of panties to sell wholesale at $10 and up, depending on how tarnished they were. As the haul grew, Mikki could offer pieces graded according to the panty's former owner, with categories like "college student," "career woman," and "prepubescent" at the top of the heap. Ikeda was ready to venture into Tokyo's market. He set up a boutique in the Takadanobaba District, and quickly made a name for himself by selling underwear that was cheaper and more besmirched than anything offered elsewhere in the metropolis, and by launching a spectacular array of badly soiled nurses' uniforms.

Ikeda opened one *chūko shitagi-ten* (secondhand underwear outlet) after another, five by 1993. They were all strategically located near train stations, thus adding to the roster of his clients the hordes of provincial connoisseurs who would ride into town for a hasty and discreet bout of shopping. Young girls soon realized that there were career opportunities in panty-soiling. In a matter of hours a dexterous worker could prepare stacks of panties, earning what a secretary might earn in a week. But in December, 1992, in an interview with the magazine *Asahi Geinō*, Ikeda pointed out that selling used panties was not a simple matter. Panty-fanatics being what they are, they could not be sold just anything. A specialist, he claimed, could tell a soiled high school specimen from that of a college student with no more than a perfunctory glance. As a result, only the deftest teenage suppliers could churn out panty after panty with the authentic four-day look that connoisseurs would pay hard cash for.

Soon other stores opened, each prized by enthusiasts for its specialty. Atene, for instance, in Tokyo's Ueno District, is known for its selection of used bras, which are offered alongside leather and rubber wear, and what the sales assistant promotes as *homoseihin* (homosexual articles). Ado and Poshetto, two sister boutiques in Nagoya City, pride themselves in their grubby schoolgirl sock collection. Q-Tii in Higashi Ikebukuro in Tokyo offers splotched stewardess uniforms, and Tifany in the Shibuya District sells everything from tattered aerobics outfits to used G-strings. Rope, in Tokyo's Takadanobaba District, goes even further. It caters to those known in the trade as the *sērāfuku mania* (sailor-suit maniac). This is the connoisseur who eagerly collects soiled *sērāfuku*—pretty, navy-collared Japanese schoolgirl uniforms. To stimulate his imagination, every outfit comes with a demure picture of its former owner. In an interview with the magazine *Za Besuto* (The Best) in January 1993, Rope's proprietor commented on how the most prized uniforms in stock were those of Japan's elite high schools. A Seishin Jogakuin uniform can go for ¥98,000—over $900.

The Tokyo customer who might be interested in even more variety can turn to Ai near the Mánseibashi police station, or walk a mile west to Yūyū, a boutique at 701 Happy Hongō in the Bunkyo District. These places offer not only the run-of-the-mill panties and high-school uniforms, but also feature heavily used sportswear like dance leotards and blotchy tennis skirts, and, for older clients, bloomers, threadbare garter straps, and corsets.

Many of the largest panty boutiques prefer to call themselves *otona no omochaya* (adult toy stores) or more elegantly, *baraieti shoppu* (variety shops). To draw mainstream customers they display hot items like variable-speed vibrators, inflatable dolls (male and female), erectile creams, nipple-exciters, wigs, and aphrodisiacs. The first-timer visiting these boutiques soon realizes that nothing is quite what it seems. What strikes the eye immediately upon entering are the lines of dildos that are disguised in their packages to look like dolls with smiling faces painted on. The new Anti-Porn Laws of 1985 forced the adult toy manufacturers to camouflage all produce that might offend a sensitive eye. As a result, the browser might pick up an endearing little toy boot, and gasp, quickly replacing it on the shelf, as he reads, "Insert penis in hole, switch on to desired speed." Even more astonishing are the shelves of children's dolls with frilly skirts and fluffy hair. These are just under a foot tall and can be placed on a sideboard without arousing anyone's suspicion. But, insert two Walkman batteries, drag down their panties, and apply lubricant, and they can climax male organs within seconds.

Some of the most successful items on sale are the life-size dolls. AIDS awareness, many adult boutique owners claim, has driven bachelors and overnight businessmen into spending billions of yen on the newest "Dutch wife" models. One of the cheapest editions is the Love Doll, retailing at $70. It is inflatable, has an electric vagina, comes with its own panties, and is an effigy of the triple-X actress, Sakuragi Rui. On the other side of the scale is the $450 Local Housewife model (*osanazuma*). She weighs only four pounds, can be folded to fit into an overnight bag, and can easily be assembled into a haunching position. Clients who are prepared to pay even more, can purchase dolls from Harumi Design's Kindan Rorikon (prohibited Lolita complex) series. Sachiko, 16, is available at $550, and her even younger sister, Michiko, despite her tender years, specializes, according to her label, in sodomy. (Harumi Designs even offers a special two-foot toddler-sized dummy).

Today's thriving adult toy trade developed from the murky underground networks of the fifties and early sixties. The term *otona no omocha* (adult toy) is said to have been invented by one Ōtsubo Naoki, who in September of 1968 opened the mother of modern triple-X boutiques, Dageru. In those days the adult toy trade was still in its infancy. Eight-millimeter porn films were heavily censored, pictures were blotted with india ink, dildos were made of painfully rough rubber that could not stand up to boisterous usage. Popular gadgets such as organ-enlargers and pocket-vaginas were considered so hot that they had to be sold under the counter, along with used panties and the naughtier playing cards. If a shop assistant so much as said "vibrator!" to an undercover agent, he would be dragged off to the precinct, the boutique closed down and the owner fined, and, if he had a record, even put in jail.

But Ōtsubo stood up for his rights. Within two months of opening Dageru he was raided by a police squad from the Azabu District and locked up for 15 days for selling off-color pictures. No sooner was he out than he succumbed to a second raid, this time by a Ueno District squad—20 days. Then, when a fellow boutique in Asakusa was invaded and the officers found a pile of kinky pictures with Dageru stamped on them, Ōtsubo was slapped with a 22-day sentence. He protested loudly, refused to cooperate, and as a result was held in a detention center for 60 days. No sooner was he released than he was attacked by a squad from the Atago District, and then one from the distant province of Akita (where he was doing business), and then back in Tokyo by a squad from the Ogikubo precinct. According to Hasegawa Takuya in his book *Saikin no Waisetsu Shuppan*, Ōtsubo was arrested altogether 31 times during those turbulent years as a pornographic pioneer.

PHOTOGRAPHS AND ILLUSTRATIONS

INDEX

ABOUT THE AUTHOR

Born in London and brought up in Austria and Greece, **Peter Constantine** was trained in ballet and performed professionally. He now writes and translates full time in German, Greek, Russian, Afrikaans, Dutch, and French, in addition to English. He makes his home in New York, and is fast becoming an expert in the field of Japanese slang and the subcultures that use it.